# The Financial Shepherd
## Why Dollars + Change = Sense

Glen Wright, II and Sy Pugh
TheFinancialShepherd.com

*AuthorHouse™*
*1663 Liberty Drive*
*Bloomington, IN 47403*
*www.authorhouse.com*
*Phone: 1-800-839-8640*

© 2011 Glen Wright, II and Sy Pugh. All rights reserved.

No part of this book may be reproduced, stored in a retrieval system, or transmitted by any means without the written permission of the author.

First published by AuthorHouse     09/16/2011

ISBN: 978-1-4634-0494-9 (sc)
ISBN: 978-1-4634-0492-5 (ebk)

Library of Congress Control Number: 2011907292

Printed in the United States of America

Any people depicted in stock imagery provided by Thinkstock are models, and such images are being used for illustrative purposes only. Certain stock imagery © Thinkstock.

This book is printed on acid-free paper.

Because of the dynamic nature of the Internet, any web addresses or links contained in this book may have changed since publication and may no longer be valid. The views expressed in this work are solely those of the author and do not necessarily reflect the views of the publisher, and the publisher hereby disclaims any responsibility for them.

*All names have been changed to protect client confidentiality.

# The Financial Shepherd:
## Why Dollars + Change = Sense
### by Glen Wright, II, CFP and Sy Pugh, LPC

| | |
|---|---:|
| Introduction | 1 |
| Chapter 1 – Money Mistakes Many People Make | 9 |
| Chapter 2 – The Unlikely American Dream | 17 |
| Chapter 3 – The Foundation of the Financial Shepherd | 23 |
| Chapter 4 – The Importance of Wise Counsel | 31 |
| Chapter 5 – The Warning Signs of Financial Failure | 42 |
| Chapter 6 – Is the Mirror Broken, Or Am I? | 49 |
| Chapter 7 – The Battle for Financial Freedom | 58 |
| Chapter 8 – Plan Your Financial Future | 68 |
| Chapter 9 – Your Financial Plan is Personal | 79 |
| Chapter 10 – Invest in Yourself | 98 |
| Chapter 11 – Planning for Retirement | 112 |
| Chapter 12 – Life Has Its Challenges, Be Prepared | 123 |
| Chapter 13 – Hope for the Best, Plan for the Worst | 132 |
| Chapter 14 – Blessed to Be a Blessing | 141 |

## Authors' Preface and Statement of Purpose

Dear Friend,

*By writing this book, it is our intent to help the readers of* The Financial Shepherd *overcome the obstacles of financial despair that may prevent them from living a fruitful and fulfilling life. Our goals include helping the reader become a better steward of God's gifts while also becoming a Financial Shepherd. Our hope is that these learned principles will not be limited solely to financial status or gain, but will be manifested and applied to one's daily life. Our desire is to ultimately give all praise, honor, and glory to our Lord and Savior Jesus Christ.*

Grace and Peace to you,

Glen Wright II, CFP
Financial Shepherd

Sy Pugh, LPC
Financial Shepherd

# Acknowledgments

To my loving wife, Kisha, thank you for your patience and continuous support. I look forward to forever with you.

To Pastor Barton Harris, senior pastor of Westwood Baptist Church Nashville Tennessee, and Mary Anne Howland, CEO of IBIS Communications, thank you for your contributions in making this project a reality.

To Dr. Peggy Enochs, special thanks for all your hard work and support in this endeavor.

Glen Wright


To my lovely bride Nichole and my sweet inspirations Sydney and Nicholes - Love you!!!

Special thanks to: Dr. John Munro and my Calvary Church Charlotte North Carolina family; my Men's Priority Group; Mrs. Jennifer P. Davis; and Phi Nu Pi.

Sy Pugh

# Introduction

Have you ever wondered why some people have SO much money, and why others have so little? What makes the super-rich any different from you? For anyone who has ever wondered what the difference is between the "haves" and the "have-nots," you may have just found your answer. Regardless of how much money you have or don't have, the journey to financial success begins with understanding and accepting how you think about money, how you feel about money, and what you know about money. Once you achieve a realistic assessment of where you are financially, there are specific steps and proven strategies that can propel you toward accomplishing positive financial goals and securing financial freedom.

Dollars + Change = Sense is the equation for financial success. This subtitle is based on the idea that it makes sense to change your old financial habits if you aren't in a desirable financial position or if you'd like to improve your current financial situation and maximize opportunities to increase wealth. The "Dollars" represent your current assets and liabilities, financial strengths and weaknesses, and other tools and resources that can be used to implement a good financial plan. "Change" represents your attitude and willingness to learn new information and apply new methods of financial management taught or demonstrated by professionals in the financial arena. "Sense" implies a reliable ability to judge and make good decisions as a result of training, maturity, and experience. Prepare to abandon old habits and adopt a new way of thinking about money. It is time to take control of your finances and embrace savvy new ways to spend, save, and invest in your financial future.

If you browse the shelves at any library or bookstore, you will see there are many books written on finance. Some are written from a Christian perspective, some deal with feelings about spending and emotional attachments to money, others deal primarily with financial terminology and the technical aspects of money management. Many purport to be "how to" books that teach the reader tricks of the trade and how to "get rich quick." But this book is designed to help readers identify real problems in their own finances and to provide real solutions that work.

Throughout the entire book, you will be given guidelines for completing a basic financial assessment, understanding key financial terms, identifying a reputable financial planner, working with licensed professionals and counselors, developing and following a financial plan, achieving long-term investment, retirement and estate planning goals, and discovering God's ultimate financial plan for your life. It may be useful to highlight specific terms or concepts, take notes in the margins, and re-read certain sections to make sure you not only read the information, but comprehend it as well. Realize that undergoing a financial transformation not only takes skill, but it also takes time. Making a commitment to understand, adjust, and improve your financial habits is one of the most important investments you will ever make, and it is guaranteed to offer a good return. The Financial Shepherd will help lead you up the path of financial recovery or down the road toward financial independence.

> $$$ **Money Matters Tip:** Look for important Money Matters throughout the book, highlighted by large dollar-sign symbols $$$ to get your attention. When you see these symbols, take a moment to study and absorb the information because it explains an important financial principle or recommends additional tools and resources that you will want to include in your own financial planning and investment strategies.

As co-authors, we've chosen to combine our experience in counseling and financial planning –including more than 2,500 interviews with clients and people discussing finances and countless hours of research and study—to understand and know what works and what doesn't work. We want to share that information with you!

Glen's role as a Certified Financial Planner (CFP), Registered Financial Consultant (RFC), and Registered Investment Advisor means that he typically works with and solves financial problems for well-to-do people who can afford his services. But what about the people who can't? What about the people who don't have room in their budgets to secure the support of professional resources to help them achieve their financial goals?

This book is for them and allows them to have access to the same assistance and guidance that wealthy people have, in addition to gaining new skills to help achieve their financial aspirations.

Typically, Sy's role as a licensed therapist is often viewed with skepticism and resistance due to the various types of stigmas frequently associated with counseling, therapy, and psychoanalysis. Many times individuals or families who seek out counseling support are labeled as "weak" or "privileged" - as if only people with more money than problems can sometimes lose their way. The truth is, we all lose our way at some point and need someone to help us get back on the right track. When it comes to money: how we think about it, how we feel about it, how much access we've had to it, and our history with it, can create serious emotional attachments, ideologies, and behaviors related to how we manage money throughout our lives. By the last chapter, you should have acquired more insight into your own emotional quotient and emotional attachment to money and have a better understanding of why you spend, save, or invest the way you do. You also will come away with new ways to think about how to change your current financial habits for the better.

In this book, we will show readers not just how to get out of debt and generate more income, but also how to use the lessons and financial tools they discover to follow God's financial plan for abundance, prosperity, and wealth. Consider adding this book to both your home and office libraries and using it as a financial training tool for your children or teenagers to properly equip them for increased financial responsibilities. Once you've mastered the enclosed content, prepare to share and mentor others and help break the cycles of generational debt and financial bondage that are so common in our society. Be encouraged to take the information you learn and help uplift others by "paying it forward", a concept defined as selflessly passing along goodwill to others. We want to put you on the path to becoming a Financial Shepherd and mentoring others to become financial leaders as well. Financial Shepherds are individuals who are knowledgeable and experienced with making good financial decisions. They are blessed to be a blessing, meaning they have the privilege of wealth and abundance to provide for their own households, and enough to give and share with others while passing along their knowledge, wisdom, and experience to the next generation. Financial Shepherds guide others to financial independence, and they lead by example.

Throughout your journey toward financial independence you will undoubtedly meet and connect with some impressive individuals who are willing to share with you their secrets and stories of success. Learn from them, and value the role they play in your life. In contrast, you're also likely to encounter some rather unsavory characters who have nothing to lose, but everything to gain by misleading or exploiting you and taking advantage of any opportunity you give them. These individuals may come in the form of financial charlatans offering gimmicks and hot tips that sound too good to be true. You can learn from them too, but it's more beneficial to avoid them or completely dismiss them from your circle of influence. As you proceed toward financial freedom, here are some of the characters to avoid along the way. Beware of:

*Imposters* – These individuals have titles and talk a good game, but they don't have the knowledge, training, or resources to take you where you want to go. Although they may look the part, talk the talk, and show up at all the right places, Imposters tend to be a mile wide, but about an inch deep. They have no depth of wisdom or experience, and they haven't yet accomplished the things they say they can do for you. This is dangerous because it's a basic rule that you cannot teach what you do not know.

*The Shiny Suit Man* – This individual is solely out to get what he (or she) wants for himself at any cost. He may look good on the outside and leave a lasting first impression, but danger lurks beneath the surface because things are not what they seem. Much like an Imposter, he talks a good game, but he's deceptively slick and borders on being ruthless, unethical, and immoral in his dealings. People like this are opportunists. They run scams on the elderly, capitalize on con games, stalk widows or widowers to marry them for their money, and then disappear. They routinely set up fraudulent companies and offer services they cannot provide, while asking for up-front fees, and then they vanish before the work is done. Shiny Suits tend to leave a trail of financial destruction in their wake, so beware!

*Wolf in Sheep's Clothing* – The Biblical inference for this individual is someone who appears to be friendly and supportive, but inwardly means you no good. Unfortunately, the pursuit of money tends to bring out the absolute worst in some people. So make sure you know the character and integrity of the professionals you hire to represent you. Make sure they have your best interest at heart and aren't just wolves in sheep's clothing out to do you harm.

An African proverb famously quotes, "When there is no enemy within, the enemy outside cannot hurt you." Many people are facing financial difficulties because they are their own worst enemy. They are reaping what has already been sown in the form of unrestrained debt and reckless spending, and are now suffering the consequences of their own choices. Ultimately, financial success will result from abandoning poor financial practices, learning and applying good financial habits, and consistently making wise decisions based on reliable and credible information from reputable professionals.

You will learn a lot more from this book if you approach it with an open mind and entertain the idea that there are some thoughts, beliefs, and perceptions you have about money that might be hindering your financial growth. Generally speaking, there are numerous persistent myths and misconceptions about money that we should address from the start, including *Money Mistakes Many People Make* (see Chapter 1) and *The Warning Signs of Financial Failure* (see Chapter 5) which includes a section on "The Top 5 Irrational Thoughts About Money."

One of the most common misconceptions that we encounter is based on how people have been taught to think about money. Many individuals—especially Christians—feel that money or the pursuit of money is an evil, negative activity. As a matter of fact, they have been led to believe that money is bad and that it should not play a significant role in the lives of fellow Christian believers. There is absolutely no truth to this way of thinking, because it is clear that money plays a crucial role in our livelihood and basic survival here on earth. As a matter of fact, there are more scriptures in the Bible about money than there are about heaven and hell, so clearly, it must be important. Let's clear up a couple of misconceptions right now.

Lesson No. 1: Money is neither good nor bad; it is neutral. The use of money and how it is applied or spent is characteristic of the individual or organization that controls the money. So the bottom line is that it isn't money that's good or bad, it's the person who has it and whether he or she chooses to use it for good or bad purposes.

Lesson No. 2: It's true that the *love* of money is the root of all evil, but it's also true that the proper use of money can be the key to lifelong and generational wealth providing safety, stability, blessings, and opportunities to pursue countless endeavors for the glory of God. Like every other aspect of our lives, God has established rules of order for acquiring, managing, and distributing our finances. The Bible should be our first, foremost, and final authoritative guide on how to think about money and how to use money for our own lives and the lives of others within our sphere of influence.

Evident in both the Old and New Testaments, the role and uses of resources and money are clearly articulated. What is consistently clear is that everything we have belongs to God, and ultimately, we are simply stewards over the gifts He has given us. From Genesis to Revelation, God mandates the principles of Working, Tithing, Financial Planning, Investing, and Giving. In the Garden of Eden, Adam was given land to tend. In the story of Cain and Abel, we see the importance of tithing from our increase—and the serious consequences of disobedience to God's commands. In the book of Luke, the question is posed whether any good steward does not first stop and "count the cost" before undertaking a particular endeavor. The parable of the talents teaches us about investing and making money grow to the glory of God. And throughout scripture, we are repeatedly taught that it is more blessed to give than to receive. It took money to build the temple of God and for King Solomon to rebuild God's house. When God wanted to bless Solomon for his genuine request for wisdom, He blessed him with land, cattle, and riches. What we can gather from these lessons is that God views money as a blessing and that He honors the responsible use of money as a tool to accomplish specific goals. God's Word underscores the importance of work and fair wages, paying tithes and taxes, not going into debt or co-signing for the debt of others, giving to the poor and supporting the work of ministry, and providing for future generations by being a good steward. In addition, the Bible clearly speaks against hoarding wealth, worshipping money, and exploiting others for gain.

Over the years, the prevalence of greed and corruption have perverted our views on money and shifted our focus from the Giver to the gift. When we lose sight of God and concentrate on getting rather than giving, then the love of money fuels a multitude of sins and other evil pursuits.

When you finish reading this book, our hope is that you will gain a new perspective on money and the role it should play in your life. We want to introduce new information about how to become financially independent according to God's Word and how to discover His financial plan for your life. We want you to have access to the same information that millionaires and billionaires have; in the process, gaining a true understanding of money and how it can be used to help you walk into your God-given destiny.

**Money Matters to God**

God has a lot to say about money. Commit to studying and memorizing some of the scriptures below and incorporate them into your family's financial planning. Additional passages of scripture are located at the end of the book. *[Scriptures are taken from the English Standard Version (ESV)]*

**Deuteronomy 8:18**
You shall remember the LORD your God, for it is he who gives you power to get wealth, that he may confirm his covenant that he swore to your fathers, as it is this day.

**Deuteronomy 15:10**
You shall give to him freely, and your heart shall not be grudging when you give to him, because for this the LORD your God will bless you in all your work and in all that you undertake.

> $$$ How you spend money is a direct reflection of the priorities in your life. Itemize the expenses in your checkbook or bank statement to get a snapshot of what's most important to you, and then use that information to realign your priorities if necessary.

**Joshua 1:8**
This Book of the Law shall not depart from your mouth, but you shall meditate on it day and night, so that you may be careful to do according to all that is written in it. For then you will make your way prosperous, and then you will have good success.

**Psalm 23:1**
The LORD is my shepherd; I shall not want.

**Psalm 37:4**
Delight yourself in the LORD, and He will give you the desires of your heart.

**Psalm 112:5**
It is well with the man who deals generously and lends; who conducts his affairs with justice.

**Proverbs 13:11**
Wealth gained hastily will dwindle, but whoever gathers little by little will increase it.

**Ecclesiastes 5:10**
He who loves money will not be satisfied with money, nor he who loves wealth with his income; this also is vanity.

**Malachi 3:10**
Bring the full tithe into the storehouse, that there may be food in my house. And thereby put me to the test, says the LORD of hosts, if I will not open the windows of heaven for you and pour down for you a blessing until there is no more need.

**Matthew 6:24**
No one can serve two masters, for either he will hate the one and love the other, or he will be devoted to the one and despise the other. You cannot serve God and money.

**Philippians 4:19**
And my God will supply every need of yours according to his riches in glory in Christ Jesus.

**Hebrews 13:5**
Keep your life free from the love of money, and be content with what you have, for he has said, "I will never leave you nor forsake you."

# Chapter I – Money Mistakes Many People Make

American author and philosopher Henry David Thoreau wrote, "If a man does not keep pace with his companions, perhaps it is because he hears a different drummer. Let him step to the music which he hears, however measured or far away." In today's words, that would translate that we should not endeavor to measure ourselves or our progress in life by the standards of others. Instead, we should follow the path that has been laid before us or better yet, blaze a new trail that best suits our needs. When it comes to managing our finances, we must be able to make tough, responsible decisions—regardless of what others around us are doing—and then accept the consequences of our actions.

One of the most effective systems of checks and balances in money management is accountability. Although most people seemingly desire to do the right things when it comes to finances, societal pressures (peers, greed, selfishness, etc.) allow them to lose focus. However, having someone ask questions and inquire about their motives makes them accountable to someone and something other than their own whims, motivations and selfish desires. Seeking out financial accountability is a crucial step to avoiding several of the money mistakes that most people make.

**Confusing Wants vs. Needs**

[Glen] When it comes to money and material things, I believe most people intuitively know what they need, and understand what they want – and why they want it. On the other hand, knowledge of such information isn't necessarily enough to compel them to take responsible action and live within their means. At the source of most financial disasters is a blurring of the lines between what is truly a need versus a want.

Understanding the difference between wants and needs and being able to patiently wait for the manifestation of either or both means that people must take responsibility and ownership solely for what God has given them. In addition, they must demonstrate faith in His ability to provide for them in His own way, and in His own time. This is often much easier said than done. The line between having what we need and getting what we want is often blurred and frequently confused. More often than not, people who cannot effectively distinguish their wants from their needs end up crossing that line and then suffering financial hardship as a result.

If we go back to the basics, food, shelter, clothing, and education are the absolute essentials for survival in modern-day society. In truth, beyond the basics, everything else is a want or simply a desire for more. But in reality, most of us can't, won't, and don't stop there, because the allure of a life of excess and indulgence is much too appealing.

Even though we affirm that food is a need, we constantly see individuals and families spend excessive amounts of money on food and dining out. Yes we need food, but we do not need gourmet dining or catered meals every night. I find that many individuals, especially single people, spend far too much money on food. Whenever I meet with a new client who is having trouble with his or her cash management, extra food and grocery expenses are usually the culprit. Because we need to eat every day, it's easy for extra food and beverage costs to sneak in throughout the day and week. Although it may be easy to budget for a weekly or monthly grocery bill, it's easy to forget how much early-morning custom coffees and midday lunches can add up. In addition, a lot of people like to eat out and splurge on the weekends, above and beyond the dining budget they have established. So now what was supposed to be a $250 budget has turned into a $600-$1,000 extravagance per month depending on the size of the family and the type of restaurants they frequent.

Ironically, I've also observed that many clients who are already on tight budgets tend to eat out even more often because they are stressed out or unhappy and spend money as a form of "therapy" to nurse their emotional wounds. They splurge and treat themselves to extra smaller perks since they cannot realistically afford to take a vacation or indulge an expensive shopping spree. No matter how big or small the expense, it is a common money mistake to think that you can consistently spend money you don't have without paying a bigger price down the road.

Without question, everyone needs somewhere to stay, but does each child really need his or her own private suite or wing in the home? It's amazing to me to hear people that grew up years ago with four brothers and sisters in a 1,400-square-foot home now tell me they need a 10,000-square-foot mansion because they have two children and one on the way. As opposed to viewing a home as a dwelling place, many families bought into the idea that they would invest in their homes and use them for financial leverage. Unfortunately for millions of people, they didn't do all the necessary research and legwork to make sure they could legitimately afford the house they purchased. There was no emergency reserve fund in place. There was no savings account, and there was no contingency plan in case one or both spouses lost their jobs. Though there are a thousand different variations of that story, the end result is often the same: failure to plan for the worst resulted in planning to fail the home ownership test. Who said that you have to own a McMansion? Who are you trying to impress… and why?

Wardrobe is another area where people tend to spend excessively. No one is questioning whether or not clean, warm clothing is essential, however designer labels are not necessities. Clothing can be a big budget buster.

I have studied books about frugal millionaires who live like paupers; eventually growing too old or decrepit to enjoy their wealth. I've also read articles and books asserting that Christians are not supposed to have, enjoy, and maintain wealth. I disagree. I believe that Christians are supposed to have all that God has made available for us. We see examples from the Old Testament to the New Testament (from Solomon's regal raiment to Jesus' seamless robe) that indicate quality clothing is important, but it has its proper place. Yes, looking good and having nice quality clothing may not be cheap, but there are things you can do to minimize wasteful spending on clothes: 1. buy sale items. 2 clip coupons 3. save where you can by spending less on general items like socks or pantyhose, or purchasing them in quantity for discount savings. If you are willing to look for a solution, there is always a way to save more money.

When it comes to money and bountiful living, I believe God wants us to cherish each day on earth and reap the benefits of His kingdom. I also understand that it takes money to see and experience many of God's gifts. I remember going on safari in South Africa and visiting the Grand Canyon in the western part of the United States. These are remarkable places, and it is evident that only God could make something so spectacular, so I was humbled by the opportunity to experience His greatness. I also remember that it took money to get to those places. It took hard, cold cash to pay for airline tickets, rental cars, luggage, food, and other trip expenses. Those things aren't free just because I'm a child of God. But when we commit to being good stewards (i.e., honoring God first with our finances, paying off debts, saving and investing for the future, and giving to others), God blesses us even more to enjoy our lives and to be a blessing to others.

I am a huge supporter and advocate for quality education at all levels. In fact, out of all four categories of expenses, education is where I believe one should give the most or make the most sacrifice. Growing up in good schools and nurturing environments certainly gives a great advantage to a child. Also, the difference in earning potential between someone who earns a high school diploma versus someone who earns a college degree is staggering. At the end of the day, investing in education almost always yields the highest return. However, just like everything, there must be limits and guides for moderation. I have seen parents over-do it in this area also. Just to make a social statement and keep up with the "Joneses," I have witnessed parents enroll their child in "the" private school in the city even when they were totally incapable of paying for the tuition costs. In one particular instance, in spite of a great secondary private school education, the child still ended up going to a community college because the parents didn't have enough money to send them to any other college. How backwards is that? There was an excellent, award-winning public school in their neighborhood where the child could have attended for free, yet the parents chose to bankrupt the family just to keep up appearances. They ultimately ended up sacrificing their child's opportunity to obtain a higher-quality, post-secondary education.

Another common money mistake that most people make is operating their household without a budget. Budgets work! Everyone needs a budget, because it is part of the basic foundation in a successful financial plan. Whether you make $10,000 per year or $10,000,000 per year, you must be a good steward over the talents and treasures to which you have been blessed. Successful financial management is not about how much money you make, it's about how much you keep, invest, and grow.

We're often asked about co-signing on loans for friends and family. Again, this is another huge money mistake that a lot of people make. Although everyone starts out with good intentions, nothing tends to complicate a relationship quicker than misunderstandings about money. Co-signing is a big no-no unless you are willing to cover the entire loan and simply give away the money. If you are not willing to do that, then do not put your name on the loan papers. I also do not encourage lending money to family and friends; instead, you should be willing to give it to them and forget about it. I have seen many families and friendships break up over a $100 loan. It's simply not worth the headache; just say NO.

The truth is that we cannot save everybody or fix all their problems. As much as we may want to help and bail them out, some people just will not do the right things, no matter how many times you try to help them. If you haven't already found out the hard way, one of the biggest financial lessons you too will learn is that you cannot help someone until they are ready to be helped.

> **$$$ Money Matters:** When it comes to family, friends, and finances, as a general rule, if you can't give it, don't lend it.

A common financial dilemma we often encounter is concerning what types of expenses are OK to pay with credit. For example, is it a good idea to pay tithes and offerings or support ministry working using a credit card? The answer is less about supporting ministry work and more about being able to pay off the entire debt each month. I think it is fine to pay everything with a credit card because it helps in tracking and monitoring expenses - as long as you are responsible and pay it off completely every month. If you cannot afford to do that, then you should not be using the card. God does not want us to be debtors, so you should not go into debt giving to the church or any other ministry. If you find yourself doing this, then most likely, your priorities are wrong and you should take other corrective measures to get your financial house in order.

We know there is a lot of information in this book that may require you to mentally and financially stretch beyond what you've done in the past. That is the point. And if you're starting out under a massive load of debt, the situation may seem impossible to reverse. But it is not. It takes time to get out of debt; especially following our plan, because we believe in saving while you are paying off your debt. Even though it takes time, we all know and understand that it is worth it in the end. Following the system and process of Financial Shepherding leads you back to being in the will of God and gaining access to His promises and financial blessings based on His Word.

> **$$$ Money Matters:** You don't pay yourself by spending money, you pay yourself by saving money - for the future.

## Living Above Your Means

[Sy] We all have in some way been impacted by the syndrome of 'keeping up with the "Joneses"' whether it is outright competing with them over new purchases or just finding out what the latest fashion trend is and getting it before "they" do. Regardless, the "Joneses" have taken full advantage of all media outlets in order to maximize the power of influence. In fact, my experience as a therapist, coach, father, and former teenager has allowed me to draw this conclusion: *the propaganda of the media is responsible for the greatest psychological warfare known to man.* This is just another way of saying that we are being brainwashed to spend money on things that some person (just like you or me) has determined to be "the in thing." Think about your wardrobe, your hairstyle, your vehicle, your home, and so on. Why did you choose that particular brand? Think about the generic packaging at Walmart versus that famous brand item. What is the one major difference? It's the appeal of the advertisement. When was the last time a generic brand of cereal had a television commercial? As people, we are so complex yet we can be deeply influenced by the simplest things. More often than not those simple things are wants, but not necessarily needs.

Next, money and communication typically top the list of problems confronting couples that come in for counseling. In the context of money mistakes most people make, poor decisions are usually the result of some other problem that is brewing beneath the surface. For example, my client Jimmy* bought a brand new model dream car to celebrate his "freedom" after a tumultuous breakup with his girlfriend of three years. He said he purchased the car because when they were living together, he used her car and he had no need to purchase one for himself. Now, to many the problem appears that the actual breakup of the relationship caused him to go out and get the car of his dreams as a means of revenge to assert his independence from her. But the problem is actually much greater than that. I met with Jimmy and his fiancée for three months prior to their breakup. The truth is that Jimmy's emotional spending was a result of an ongoing internal conflict to which he had already yielded. Jimmy did not have a car or a place of his own because of his insecurities in addition to his fiancée's admittedly controlling behaviors fueled by her own insecurities. So Jimmy retaliated in the best way he knew how; by going to get the dream car that he so desperately "needed." Overspending was his way of self-medicating and nurturing his internal wounds and insecurities. The result however was the accrual of debt he couldn't manage, which of course, created even more problems to compound the ones he already had. This is just one example of a situation that many people face.

It seems logical that everyone should be able to live within their financial means because the solution is simple: Do not spend more than you earn. But when it comes to money, logic seemingly goes out the window, and emotions, egos, desire, and pride kick in. As part of the emotional battle to control our spending and achieve financial independence, it is important for us to recognize the consequences of pursuing wants instead of needs. This is where most people hit a roadblock and fall short, attempting to thrive at the level of their wants instead of living solely on the more affordable needs. Financial success lies in our ability to correctly identify our true needs, and then make credible decisions based on our personal financial plan and the advice of wise counsel.

Simply put, our needs are the things that we require for survival and without them it is impossible to live. I *need* food to survive, but I *want* filet mignon and lobster. I *need* shoes to protect my feet, but I *want* the designer brand Allen Edmonds. Realize too that our needs can also be our wants, but our wants are not always what we need. The point here is not to say that there is anything wrong with having wants, but rather it is important to be conscious of the differences between wants and needs if we have to choose which is more important.

Along with our basic needs for survival, which are easily identifiable, we also have the need for wisdom to guide us through the process of making difficult decisions. "Listen to advice and accept instruction, that you may gain wisdom in the future" (Proverbs 19:20 ESV). It takes wisdom to separate wants and needs. And it takes wisdom to recognize and learn from poor financial decisions. As part of the equation for financial success, it makes good Sense to acknowledge that sometimes we have to ask for guidance and rely on someone else's wisdom until we can fully rely on our own. Most importantly, we have to rely on God's wisdom to help us continually make good decisions. When it comes to living within our means, distinguishing wants and needs, and understanding worthwhile pursuits, one of the most popular and relevant verses in the Bible can be found in Psalm 37:3-7a (NIV):

[3] Trust in the LORD and do good;
dwell in the land and enjoy safe pasture.
[4] Delight yourself in the LORD
and he will give you the desires of your heart.
[5] Commit your way to the LORD;

trust in him and he will do this:
⁶ He will make your righteousness shine like the dawn,
the justice of your cause like the noonday sun.
⁷ Be still before the LORD and wait patiently for him.

If we trust in the Lord, delight ourselves in the Lord, commit our ways to the Lord, and be still and wait patiently for the Lord, then His desires become our desires. In the process, His wisdom guides our direction, and His plan for us shapes the road we will travel. This is the true path to avoiding the money mistakes most people make.

## Chapter 2 – The Unlikely American Dream

How do you define the American Dream? Is it making more money than you ever imagined? Is it being able to own your own home and send your children to private school? Or is it the ability to work, play, relax, and travel at your leisure? For many Americans, that coveted dream takes on many different faces, but at its core are similarities that provide an opportunity for anyone and everyone to fulfill their goals of making a good living, purchasing a home of their own, and avoiding the stress and anxiety of financial hardship. For most, that is the genesis of the American Dream.

Even in the shadow of economic recession, unprecedented national debt, corporate credit freezes, stock market volatility, record levels of unemployment, and financial uncertainty on a global scale, hope remains. For millions of people around the world still envision the day when they can make it to the United States in pursuit of the American Dream that has seduced and sustained so many for so long.

In light of where we are economically, many pose the question, 'Does the American Dream still exist?' And if so, is it available to everyone to achieve? In reality, the American Dream has changed so much from its inception, that it's hardly recognizable anymore. In the beginning, the idea was to promote a sense that everyone was entitled to a better life; not just the pursuit of life, liberty, and happiness, but a quality education, rapid ascension up the corporate ladder, frequent raises and promotions, the acquisition of property, land, and ownership of assets to provide a comfortable or luxurious lifestyle. Over a period of time, rights and privileges morphed into entitlements and greed which ultimately led to corruption and exploitation in the pursuit of more, more, more.

One of the dangers of the American Dream, as it has been redefined, is that it focuses on self, rather than others. The American Dream now represents an unrealistic set of expectations that subtly determine what is temporarily considered to be "in style." Furthermore, the American Dream does not purpose to "seek first the kingdom of God," but rather it is based on the thoughts and opinions of other people which are fickle and ever-changing. The irony of chasing this dream lies in the fact that as Americans, we pride ourselves on being different, independent, and free-thinkers; yet we've allowed a predetermined, manufactured series of fads to determine how we think and act in pursuit of our desires and dreams of happiness. Unfortunately, this new American Dream lures people into a false sense of selfish expectation that somehow, just being an American or being in America is enough validation and justification to have whatever one wants whenever one wants it – without putting in the necessary work to earn and keep it. This new American Dream has fostered in people a tendency to live above their means in competition with the neighbors, colleagues, co-workers, and friends who appear to have attained their version of the dream. As a result, countless families are suffocating under a mountain of unnecessary debt and struggling to make ends meet because of the dream that has now become a nightmare.

Affordable education used to be an accessible rung on the ladder that led to economic success and upward mobility. However, "affordable education" is a paradox in the new millennium. On average, a high school diploma guarantees nothing more than the promise of a mediocre life marked by a low-paying job in a society where minimum wage does not support an individual's ability to provide for his or her family. Across the nation, college tuition rates have outpaced salary increases, and many families simply cannot afford to educate their children without going further into debt by taking on student loans or taking out second mortgages on their homes.

Despite their best attempts, many people will never attain the American Dream because of selfishness and greed by others. Consider what the Bible has to say about the reckless pursuit of material possessions in Luke 12:15 (ESV): "*...Take care, and be on your guard against all covetousness, for one's life does not consist in the abundance of his possessions.*" Although there are many characteristics of greed, the one that seems to manifest itself in all of the others is a lack of contentment. Ironically, this may be the most difficult characteristic to embrace in all areas of our lives, simply because it is only natural for us to want more.

We live in an age where satisfaction is at a constant distance from our current state of existence. Think about the brand new top-of-the-line, 40-inch plasma TVs that were the "must have" items back in 2004. A few years ago, that TV was worth $3,000. Today it is worth only $200; and besides that, you now "need" the newest model with all of the upgrades including a built-in hard drive for DVR, online video streaming, and other unnecessary features. We failed to mention that this same high-tech, overpriced gadget is also touch-screen and doubles as a computer monitor for online video chats with your family back home which supposedly makes is a necessity. That's worth another $3,000, right? Wrong. This is when we must ask ourselves whether we're being good providers or living a life that depends on "the abundance of possessions" – which is in contrast to God's Word. One of the goals of the Financial Shepherd is to learn to be content with what God has provided and not be overcome with greed.

The traditional model that supported the infrastructure of the original American Dream no longer exists. In the past, it was built on getting a basic education, getting a job at a local company, then working your way up through the ranks, investing 25 to 30 years of hard work, dedication and loyalty, and in return, reaping the financial rewards of your success. Upon retirement, there were ample benefits, along with a well-funded government subsidy—or financial entitlements—and various investment opportunities and stock options to finance a comfortable, mortgage-free retirement. That scenario no longer exists. Historically, the fulfillment of the American Dream was built around a well-structured plan with contributions from the government, corporate America, and your own personal investments. Now, most likely, that plan mostly consists of personal and individual contributions. The reality is that you may be the only plan you have.

Most employees in the modern workforce will not only change jobs numerous times, but will change industry professions an average of four times over the tenure of their careers. Working for the same organization for the lifespan of an entire career is almost unheard of nowadays. Blue chip companies that once were the engine of the American economy have stalled and shifted their focus from people to profits – at any cost. Large corporations facing falling stock prices and antsy investors in turn bartered company pensions and employee retirement benefits to bankroll executive bonuses and pad their bottom lines. Without question, the pathway that led to the American Dream has been severely altered beyond the point of recognition.

## Redefining the American Dream

When we put things in proper perspective and realign our goals and dreams with God's plan for us, we will find that there isn't a one-size-fits-all dream that everyone is obligated to pursue. God has a plan for each of our lives, and when we spend time following His Will instead of chasing somebody else's dream, we will find that life becomes much simpler, less stressful, and much more fulfilling.

One of the questions that we're frequently asked is whether home ownership—a staple of the idealistic American Dream—is for everyone. Our answer is 'no' – for a variety of reasons. Some people simply don't earn enough to purchase a home and cover the expenses of homeowners insurance, homeowners association dues, home maintenance, home repairs, home furnishings, lawn upkeep, and the general costs of 'curb appeal' required to make sure the home maintains its property value and contributes to beautifying the neighborhood. Paying the mortgage is just one of many expenses associated with having that dream home. We've also learned that some people don't want the responsibilities that come with maintaining a home. It's just easier to write one check each month and let someone else handle the details and multitude of bills that come along with the home ownership territory. For many savvy individuals, renting or leasing their residence provides a sense of freedom that allows them to pursue other, more profitable investment ventures.

Years ago, one of our clients made a calculated financial decision and committed to renting instead of purchasing a home. Over time, he amassed great wealth because he focused on saving and investing instead of spending. When the housing market collapsed, it didn't directly affect him at all, and he was able to benefit and accumulate even more wealth while others struggled to keep from drowning in debt due to adjusting and fluctuating mortgage rates. The point of the story and the key to his success was that this individual followed God's priorities of avoiding debt and listened to the advice of wise counsel instead of following the crowd just to keep up appearances.

Another example demonstrates how the lack of knowledge about the responsibilities of home ownership can be costly and detrimental to an entire family. We have a friend whose grandmother died and left the family home to her five children. There was a small mortgage on the home which could have easily been paid off between the five siblings. Unfortunately, the surviving children gambled against the market in hopes of securing a higher sale price, but the anticipated market recovery never materialized.

In the interim, no one bothered to pay the mortgage. Missed payments, late fees, and penalties began to accrue, and now, the home is being foreclosed. The family will suffer a loss of approximately $75,000 in home equity that took years to establish. In a matter of months, a $75,000 gain that took decades to build has now resulted in more than a $100,000 total loss. In the end, the family home will be lost, the money invested in the home will be lost, and a valuable credit line and source of collateral for financial leverage will be lost because no one in the family understood the significance of responsible home ownership.

One thing we've learned is that pursuing any version of the American Dream isn't worth it if the accumulation of "stuff" is the main goal. Matthew 6:33 (KJV)—in no uncertain terms—makes our priority clear: "But seek ye first the kingdom of God, and his righteousness; and all these things shall be added." In that passage of scripture, the things that shall be added refer to clothing, sustenance, and daily provisions for living. Jesus is telling his disciples that when the focus is on Him, then they need not be concerned with how to acquire anything else. As the Apostle Paul stated in Philippians 4:19 (KJV), 'My God shall supply all your need according to His riches in glory by Christ Jesus.'

Another problem we've observed with the traditional American Dream is that its attainment is built on impossibility. The version of the American Dream that encourages everyone to buy a home, purchase a new car, and spare no expense to educate their children, also encourages them to take out a 30-year loan that ends up creating an unmanageable debt load which is top-heavy on interest rate payments; finance a vehicle that loses value within the first hour of ownership; and borrow for student loans that often inflict irreparable damage to credit histories and credit scores and negatively impact the ability to acquire new credit in the future. In essence, the unlikely American Dream we've been sold basically instructs people to finance their futures through debt, bad loans, and material possessions they cannot afford.

In the 1990s and 2000s, people who clearly couldn't afford a mortgage and didn't have the income to support home ownership were given mortgages without any regard for their income, credit history, debt-to-income ratio, or employment. These high-risk loans were issued to people who couldn't afford them because they were profitable for individuals and organizations that could: the banks, mortgage companies, investors, and underwriters. The short-term gains fueled by greed took no consideration of the long-term failures that inevitably would result. On the other end of the spectrum are individuals who could afford a modest home mortgage, but were compelled to purchase multimillion-dollar mega-mansions out of opportunistic greed and the desire to have more than the next person. Although recent headlines have shone brightly on low- to moderate-income home foreclosures, the number of foreclosures for high-end homes has been equally substantial due to the residents' inability to pay their mortgages, including many that fluctuated upwards of 80 percent due to adjustable interest rates. All across the nation, the financial rubber is meeting the economic road, and the results are sobering. People are finally waking up from the dream and facing a new reality.

The harsh lesson being learned is that you cannot spend your way out of debt. For what it's worth, the good news is that Americans are being forced to reset their priorities and at the same time are becoming more realistic in their financial planning and aspirations. The bad news is that old habits are hard to break and are very slow to change. When the example set before us is a federal government spending its way into bankruptcy, and a financial system that rewards corruption and irresponsible behavior, it's difficult to pass along better examples to citizens who are repeatedly encouraged to spend more money to support the economy. Big banks and corporations are given bailouts at the expense of everyday tax-payers who themselves are continuing to struggle. Whether we like it or not, as a nation of debt-laden consumers, the time has come to reap what we have sown. Indeed, we're realizing that the so-called American Dream is in fact a contradiction of terms. Why? Because it is inherently un-American to fund your own excess at the expense of others. It is un-American to gamble away the future for the short-lived pleasures of the present. And it is un-American, unscriptural, and unwise to build your future on a shaky financial foundation that is the theoretical equivalent of sinking sand.

For those wondering how to survive the current tumultuous landscape, the answers can be found first in the Bible and in your own private prayer life to seek God's wisdom and guidance about your financial situation. The best advice for achieving God's will for your life can be found in the verse of Hebrews 13:5 (NIV) which states, "Keep your lives free from the love of money and be content with what you have", because God has said, "Never will I leave you; never will I forsake you." The realization that God is with us and that God is for us is the best dream we can possibly ask for.

# Chapter 3 – The Foundation of the Financial Shepherd

The concept of Financial Shepherding refers to guardianship of God's abundance. Much like traditional shepherds of old, contemporary Financial Shepherds have sheep (or followers) who heed our words and actions, and follow our instruction and counsel about money. Financial Shepherds guide their followers through economic and financial pastures and assist in the nourishment, protection, and growth of the group. By definition, they gather (herd), protect (guard), and take care of (tend) the sheep. Within the Body of Christ, these individuals are the ones who oversee the tithes, talents, and treasures that belong to the kingdom and children of God.

A responsible and godly Financial Shepherd is someone who esteems others more highly than himself; not only valuing their own interests, but also protecting and serving the interests of others. These leaders make a commitment to love, serve, and provide for their own families in addition to blessing others in need. Financial Shepherds are called to be good stewards of God's resources.

**The Nature of Sheep**

Let's talk a little about the nature of real sheep and then compare it to the nature of people.

Have you ever wondered why sheep in a pasture just blindly follow the shepherd, even though he doesn't look like they do or act like they do? Ironically, even though sheep are herd animals, they intuitively follow something or someone who isn't anything like them (i.e., wolf in sheep's clothing). However, what sheep understand—that a lot of people don't—is that the true shepherd is there to lead and protect them and has their best interest at heart. Even sheep understand that the shepherd's role is to keep the wolves and other predators away. In our society, a Financial Shepherd's role is to keep the loan sharks and financial predators away. Ultimately, the shepherd has an obligation to and vested interest in the care of the sheep because he is accountable for their safety and is compensated for his success. In God's kingdom, stewardship is profitable.

Next, sheep tend to be reactive instead of proactive. They are incapable of planning ahead or anticipating hidden dangers that may pose a threat. The shepherd's job is to identify any potential threats against the sheep and then steer them in a different, less risky direction. Sheep tend to follow a mob or herd mentality. That is, what one does, the entire group will do. If one sheep near the front of the flock walks down a steep embankment, rest assured it is just a matter of time before the rest of them will follow. That same mentality is present when it comes to people making destructive financial decisions. We've termed it, 'Keeping up with the Joneses.' If the next door neighbor buys a new car, then we have to figure out how to get a new car too. If the president of the PTA or PTSA (Parent Teacher Association or Parent Teacher Student Association) goes on a cruise, then we've got to go on a cruise as well. If your best friend gets a new stereo system or high-definition, flat-screen television, then you're already planning where to hang yours on the wall. If the rest of society decides it's OK to spend more than you make and finance your livelihood on credit cards and loans, then it must be all right to do the same, regardless of the dangers associated with that lifestyle.

Have you ever heard the term "upside down in debt?" In terms of sheep and Financial Shepherding, there is a natural correlation with this phrase. Sheep are one of the few animals that are easily "cast" which means they can literally get so burdened down by the weight of their own wool, they tip over and become unable to get right-side-up on their own. How many people (perhaps you?) can you think of that are upside-down under the weight of their own poor financial decisions? The only way to rescue the sheep is for the shepherd to come along and return it to a position of right-standing. In comparison, the only way for many of us to be financially restored is to admit that, like sheep, we are lost and have gone astray and need a Financial Shepherd to help get us back on our feet again.

Sheep are notorious for getting lost. They get distracted and mindlessly wander away – often into the path of danger. For any of you familiar with farms or ranches, you know that if you release the reins on the hitches of mules or horses (or other beasts of burden), eventually they will navigate their way back home to the farm. Not so with sheep. If you leave sheep unattended for too long, they will simply wander farther and farther away and possibly never return. Lost sheep have to be found. Even the Bible confirms this in the Gospels of Matthew and Luke through the Parable of the Lost Sheep, which required the Shepherd to leave the flock in search of the one sheep that had gone astray. Upon finding the lost sheep, the Shepherd lifts it up onto his shoulders, carries it back to safety, and nurses the sheep back to health. Similarly, Financial Shepherds understand that everyone makes mistakes, and that some people need to be rescued from financial mismanagement and literally restored to financial health.

Sheep have no claws, no horns, no sharp teeth. They are basically defenseless. Sheep are not combative creatures, so as Financial Shepherds, we have an obligation not to violate or betray the trust of those who cannot protect or defend themselves. There is no telling how many lives have been destroyed due to poor or irresponsible financial counsel. Disreputable individuals have embezzled hundreds of millions of dollars by offering unsubstantiated "get-rich-quick" schemes and fooled unsuspecting followers into handing over their hard-earned money. Countless husbands, wives, doctors, lawyers, teachers, and businessmen alike have been bilked out of their retirement or life savings by trusting someone who wasn't worthy of their trust. Genuine Financial Shepherds understand that they have a greater accountability to their clients and to their profession, but especially to God.

Here's something ironic about sheep - but you might discover that it sounds vaguely familiar and true about a lot of people as well. Sheep are stubborn. Despite their inability to sustain, provide, protect, defend, or care for themselves, they are doggedly determined to go the wrong way until the shepherd intervenes and sets them back on the right course. Although traditionally sheep have been kept in pens at night for safety, they frequently search for a way out to then aimlessly wander off. Also, sheep are not necessarily strong swimmers, but they have been known to wade into shallow rivers or streams for a drink and inadvertently get soaked from the surrounding currents. Unfortunately, when their wool gets wet, it weighs them down, and then the sheep runs the risk of drowning because it cannot support the excess water weight. And even after being rescued, it is not uncommon to find them in the exact same predicament again. In striking comparison, a common tendency of people is to keep making the same mistakes again and again, despite advice, education, instruction, workshops, books, manuals, classes, programs, and courses about demolishing debt or gaining financial freedom. But people in debt, much like stubborn sheep, are committed to following their own destructive path, only to need rescuing by the shepherd.

Finally, sheep do not like to be sheared or shaven, much like people do not like their finances to be analyzed, pruned, or restricted. Sheep will run, kick, or bleat loudly to protest being freed of the very wool that has caused them to itch, collect lice and fleas, and practically drown. As for the theoretical sheep still avoiding their Financial Shepherd, they continue to spend uncontrollably, live beyond their means, and ignore their credit reports – despite the severe consequences and the fact that those habits are robbing them and their families of a successful financial future. They often resist change or help even though it is readily available. Truthfully, a lot of people do not want to change their financial habits or how they manage their **Dollars**. They want a different outcome, but are unwilling to **Change** their minds, change their ways, make better decisions, or develop new financial habits by doing things that make **Sense**. In essence, it's insanity, which is often anecdotally defined as "doing the same thing over and over again and expecting different results."

### The Nature of Shepherds

Similar to shepherds of real sheep, Financial Shepherds share common traits in that they have a deep love and level of concern for those under their guidance and care. In both instances—literal and theoretical—shepherds understand the sheep, know what the sheep want and need to keep them healthy and safe, and also construct discipline and correction for the sheep in regard to their best interest.

One of the most crucial roles a shepherd fulfills in his care of the sheep is making sure they do not blindly follow each other into the path of destruction e.g. fall in a ditch, run off a cliff, or drown in a river. Have you ever heard someone refer to a group as "a bunch of sheep?" What that really means is that the individuals who make up the group are deemed incapable of making their own decisions or following an independent course of action. They, like sheep, are in need of a shepherd to instruct them on where to go and what to do. Consistent with God's word and His loving kindness toward us, we must be mindful of the need to end our methods and patterns of mindless conformity with the world and allow God to lead us toward His destiny for us.

Financial Shepherds are not just people who are good with money. There are countless individuals who have made wise financial investments, but have not been good stewards or shepherds to those around them. As a little boy, I remember watching close relatives who were great with saving money and successfully living well below their financial means. They saved thousands of dollars in the bank and then followed a tip from a financial advisor and began purchasing and investing in real estate. As a result, they made even more money. Unfortunately, in the process of building their fortune, they manipulated and used their friends to get ahead, and gave nothing back in return. Even though they had the opportunity to be good Financial Shepherds and educate other members in our family about how to become successful, they never did. Now, in spite of the fact that they have a lot of money, they don't have any friends or any good relationships with their family. "For what does it profit a man to gain the whole world and forfeit his soul? For what can a man give in return for his soul?" (Mark 8:36-37 ESV).

Metaphorically speaking in scripture references, Shepherd is a term used for God or His Son Jesus the Christ, who referred to Himself in John 10:11 as The Good Shepherd. Also, consider Psalm 23 in the Bible:

*The Lord is my shepherd, I shall not be in want. He makes me lie down in green pastures, he leads me beside quiet waters, he restores my soul. He guides me in the path of righteousness for his name's sake. Even though I walk through the valley of the shadow of death, I will fear no evil, for you are with me; your rod and staff, they comfort me. You prepare a table before me in the presence of my enemies. You anoint my head with oil; my cup overflows. Surely goodness and love will follow me all the days of my life, and I will dwell in the house of the Lord forever (Psalm 23 NIV).*

As our provider – and the Good Shepherd – our Heavenly Father provides everything we need. This is true whether we're discussing oxygen, healing, or food on the table. Our God is able to provide all our need – according to His riches in glory. For true believers who are followers of Christ, not just believers in Christ, there is no lack to those that love and serve Him.

So, how does someone transition from being a sheep to becoming a Financial Shepherd? Well although our stories will differ, my journey to becoming a Financial Shepherd had three pathways: 1) past financial history and upbringing; 2) education and training; and 3) divine inspiration.

## A Glimpse from the Past

[Glen]    It seems like just yesterday… but 1987 was the worst year of my life. I was 11 years old, my parents were getting a divorce, our newly divided family was struggling for money, and I was not handling it well at all.

Despite my mother's strength, wisdom, independence, and education—including a Master's degree in Theology—at the end of the day, she was still a single mother trying to figure out how to make ends meet.

As I watched the only life I had known fade into the distance, and experienced an unwelcome new reality filled with fear, disappointment, transition, doubt, and the devastation of not having enough of anything, I learned a lesson that would serve me well, and ultimately led me to my current career as a financial advisor. At age 11, I realized that regardless of your age, race, class, background, education, or status, if you don't have control over your own finances, then you don't have any control at all.

For the first decade of my life, I had grown up in what seemed to be an ideal, two-parent home where Dad was the primary breadwinner and chief financial engineer. Mom was the primary homemaker, caretaker, and nurturer with an income that was secondary to his; and as long as nothing ever changed, then everything would be OK. But things did change, and everything wasn't OK.

There's an old saying that the only constant is change. It's true. But if you don't prepare and plan for change, then you are accepting financial defeat before the battle even begins. I decided to prepare myself by going to school, getting the appropriate certifications and degrees, and changing the way I thought about money. I acknowledged and embraced the idea that until I took control of my own financial destiny—in Christ—that my life would never be my own.

I accepted early on in my walk with the Lord that I would endeavor to know and embrace His word and His will for my life. One of the first and most enduring lessons I learned was that it is God's will for His children to be blessed; for all the promises of God in Him are yea, and in Him, Amen. But I also realized that my future was not solely God's responsibility. I had to do my part too. Once I understood this principle, there was no question in my mind about God's position on money. The real question was, 'How does God want me to handle the finances and abundance that He blesses me with?'

I learned that most people give money too much credit and associate it with values it simply does not possess. For years, parents, preachers, and Sunday school teachers have misquoted the same famous passage of scripture, often stating that "money is the root of all evil," when in reality the Bible states in Ecclesiastes that money is a [defence] or asset and answers all things; while "the *love* of money is the root of all evil." The irony of finances within Christianity is that everything belongs to God, yet at some point almost everyone manages their money like it only belongs to them.

## Live and Learn... Then Keep Learning

I have accepted my role in life as a Financial Shepherd because it's one of the gifts in which God has graced me. But like any other calling in ministry, my abilities as a financial steward had to begin at home and be pruned and nurtured to where they are now. Like everyone else, I was (and still am) a work in progress.

I graduated from the University of Memphis with a degree in Finance. I also completed an 18-month financial planning curriculum which allowed me to become licensed as a Certified Financial Planner. I later earned certifications as a Registered Financial Consultant and Registered Investment Advisor. Despite my academic and professional accomplishments, I still recognize that it is my commitment to the Lord that has made all the difference. By the grace of God, I am now one of the most highly credentialed financial planners in the country, and I want to share my gift with the masses.

BUT... I remember a period of time in my life where I just made some bad financial decisions. There was a time when I used to literally trade in my car every year for a brand new model. I had just graduated from college and was earning a six-figure income, but still had nothing but a load of mounting debt to show for it. I spent $50,000 in four years on car payments from leasing and buying new cars, which is one of the absolute worst investments you can make due to the high level of depreciation or loss in value. It took years before I came to my senses and realized what a destructive pattern I was establishing. Finally, after losing a lot of time—and even more money—I picked out a vehicle, paid for it in cash, and kept it for the next seven years.

One of the best financial decisions I ever made was acquiring a credit card in college and using it to build my credit. I got in the habit of paying the entire bill on time every month for years. As time went on, I received rebates and reward points and built a solid credit history. I still have that credit card today, and now my limit is high enough to purchase a new home with it. The greatest lesson I learned from that experience was that using credit wisely can be a powerful tool for financing your future dreams and aspirations.

My own personal journey has brought me to this point. Now my role as a financial planner is to help clients grow and protect their financial assets. For more than a decade, I have built a business out of earning people's trust and educating them about wealth creation and wealth management. More important than my credentials however, is my relationship with Christ and my obligation to serve Him and His followers in a manner that glorifies God.

## Chapter 4 – The Importance of Wise Counsel

At the end of this book, in the Top 50 Financial Terms section, we define what to look for when identifying **Wise Counsel**: advice, information, warning, direction, suggestions, recommendations, caution, guidance, or admonition that provides direction as to a decision or course of action or in setting standards or determining a course of action. When it comes to finances, rarely does Wise Counsel come in the form of friends and family who haven't been professionally trained as financial planners or licensed counselors to help you face or navigate some of life's more complex issues. If your money and your children's futures are on the line, it is worth investing the time and energy to locate quality, well-trained, certified individuals who have some level of accountability for properly handling your money and money-related matters.

A good place to start is with referrals from respected individuals whose judgment you trust. Be prepared to ask a lot of questions and take notes to identify reputable financial planners and counselors in your area. It's also worthwhile to research the recommendations of various professional associations such as the Financial Planning Association, the National Association of Personal Financial Advisors, the American Institute of Certified Public Accountants, and the National Board for Certified Counselors.

Licensure is the key when looking for a qualified counselor/therapist. Be mindful that the terms counselor and therapist are often used interchangeably. In fact, the terms themselves can be related to many other areas outside the intended use in this book. People without any specified skill sets are calling themselves counselors and therapists. For example, there are credit counselors and massage therapists. Neither of these two jobs requires the licensure process that identifies the service provider as a counselor/therapist that is highly skilled and trained in this area of expertise. The difference in the use of the term and the actual discipline is the licensure and the stringent requirements that are needed to obtain and maintain such licensure. This licensure comes with a governing body by which ethical guidelines are provided and enforced. This licensure also tells the consumer that this person, at the very least, completed a master's degree program from an accredited university. Among professional groups, a Licensed Professional Counselor (LPC), Licensed Clinical Social Worker (LCSW) or Licensed Psychological Associate (LPA), are good resources that should be considered when seeking wise counsel to help guide you and your family through uncertain or challenging situations.

[Glen] The Bible says in Proverbs 11:14 (KJV), "Where there is no counsel, the people fall; but in the multitude of counselors there is safety." As a certified financial planner with a firm that has vast resources, I could help my clients with their banking needs. However, I feel that it would be a disservice to my clients because that is not my expertise. Keep in mind that your financial planner should act as the quarterback for your team and pass the ball to the appropriate receiver at the right time – with no interceptions. Remember, ultimately, you are the owner of the team, so make sure you have the right players on your squad.

**When seeking wise financial counsel, there are several things to look for:**
1. Seek Direction- It is important to make sure you have a goal and a course to follow. There are many "product pushers" trying to sell you something because they were trained and required to do so, but you have to determine if it makes sense for your individual plan. There needs to be a clear course of how your journey will lead to achieving your financial goals. I remember my first office space was a shell and I didn't see how everything was going to be able to fit into this space. However, when I met with the architect, she showed me how everything would fit and in addition, exceeded my expectations from cost, size, and time standpoints. I needed her to show me a plan that would fit my goals and she did – because that was her expertise, not mine. After our meeting, I was confident that everything would be fine although we discussed things that I knew little about. Based on her expertise and her ability

to communicate with me, I realized that I was headed in the right direction.
2. Seek Quality- The person needs to know more than you about a particular area of expertise, otherwise, you could do it on your own. The individual should have more than just training from a company, but also should have some type of designation. There are many designations that advisors can simply pay a fee for and have it on paper to make them look more credible. You want to make sure that they have accreditation and designations where extensive training and continuing education are involved. Within the financial realm, the most creditable designation is the CFP, or Certified Financial Planner. In addition, if someone is going to manage your money, they should also be a registered investment advisor. Another designation is the RFC which stands for Registered Financial Consultant and requires more continuing education than most others. Regarding finances, the point is not just about getting a designation, it's about continuing to learn and evolve as the financial world around us evolves. If you want to hire an accountant, then they need to be a signed fiduciary, or a Certified Public Accountant (CPA). If you need an attorney, make sure that individual specializes in the area of law that you need. For instance, you should not use a personal injury attorney to complete your estate planning or a defense attorney to close your real estate transactions.

Most people think that all financial planners are "certified," but this isn't true. Anyone can call himself or herself a "financial planner." Only those who have fulfilled the certification and renewal requirements of the CFP Board can display the CFP® certification marks. When selecting a financial planner, you need to feel confident that the person you choose to help you plan for your future is competent and ethical. The CFP® certification provides that sense of security by allowing only those who meet the following requirements the right to use the CFP® certification marks.

Here is some helpful information to know: CFP® professionals must develop their theoretical and practical financial planning knowledge by completing a comprehensive course of study at a college or university offering a financial planning curriculum approved by the CFP Board. CFP® practitioners must pass a comprehensive two-day, 10-hour CFP®

Certification Examination that tests their ability to apply financial planning knowledge in an integrated format. Based on regular research of what planners do, the exam covers the financial planning process, tax planning, employee benefits and retirement planning, estate planning, investment management, and insurance. Finally, CFP® professionals must have three years minimum experience in the financial planning process prior to earning the right to use the CFP® certification marks. As a result, CFP® practitioners possess financial counseling skills in addition to financial planning knowledge. As a final step to certification, CFP® practitioners agree to abide by a strict code of professional conduct, known as CFP Board's *Code of Ethics and Professional Responsibility,* that sets forth their ethical responsibilities to the public, clients and employers. The CFP Board also performs a background check during this process, and each individual must disclose any investigations or legal proceedings related to their professional or business conduct. *(Certified Financial Planner – Board of Standards, Inc. website. www.cfp.net)*

3. Seek Relationship- It is vital that you are able to communicate with your planner. A financial planner can only help you as much as he or she knows what the real problems or challenges are. I remember meeting with a couple that owned huge accounts, boasted great index investment strategies, and they assured me everything else was in order. However, that was not the case. The husband had a terminal illness, and the couple did not have proper life insurance coverage in place. They mistakenly thought their policy for accidental insurance was the same as life insurance and they did not bring in the necessary paperwork to be examined. Their limited knowledge about the industry and their failure to provide full disclosure to me as their planner proved costly. Unfortunately, the husband passed away, and upon review of their assets, it became evident that the wife didn't have proper insurance coverage for expenses or enough money to maintain her quality of life because she was only 40 and was many years away from retiring. Situations like that can be avoided if you use wisdom in seeking and building a relationship of mutual trust with your advisors.

When selecting a financial planner, it is important to make sure that you have someone who is going to listen to your problems, needs, and concerns. Because this person will have private knowledge of your finances and family matters, make sure it's someone who is competent, but also cares enough to provide the best solutions for your family needs.

Just because someone has the title of financial planner or advisor doesn't mean they have your best interest at heart. It also does not mean they have any real education or expertise in the industry. Although industry regulators are working to change this, they are not there yet. *Therefore, these same professionals that you seek to put on your team or Board of Directors should be signed fiduciaries, proving security for you with a system of legal and judicial accountability.* Your accountant needs to be a CPA. Your attorney is designated a signed fiduciary when he or she passes the state bar exam, and your financial planner needs to be a CFP which makes her or him one as well. Signed fiduciaries have an ethical and legal obligation to act in the best interest of you, the client. It is perfectly acceptable to interview several professionals before signing a contract or entering into any specific agreement. As a matter of fact, it is highly recommended that you do so. Be prepared to ask questions and take notes. Remember these tips during the interview process and weigh the pros and cons of working with each individual before making a final decision.

1. No one works for free. You need to know how much you're paying upfront and for what you are paying. No one seems to know what they are paying for these days and I find that many advisors don't disclose what you are paying in fees and/or what they are making. Have you ever read a prospectus? Those are the huge books that are purposely (in my opinion) made to intimidate the average investor. You can find all the fees that companies have to disclose and even find out the ones that do not have to be disclosed in there.
    a. My wealthy clients were referred by wealthy clients. They typically have access to the top wealth managers and get the best fees, private banking rates, etc... But normally "middle America" and less affluent people are referred to advisors and have to hope for the best. Although there are "shiny suits" in every category, I see less affluent people getting abused the most by paying excessive fees. It's true that you get what you pay for, but make sure you aren't just throwing money away – and getting nothing in return.
        i. Don't do what's popular, do what's right for you. It's amazing how uncommon things

often tend to make the most sense. Consider index funds, which do not require money managers. They are less expensive than actively managed funds. They are not widely talked about because financial firms make a lot more money conducting trading themselves, although most of them can't outperform their index benchmark for extended periods of time. It's OK to take the road less traveled, especially if it's going to make you accomplish your financial goals faster.

    ii. Fees for plans. Paying a fee is a good thing. There are many "advisors" who say they will not charge you a fee and will complete your plan for free. Remember, when it comes to managing money, there is no free ride. Those same advisors probably already know what they are going to sell you even before you get started. It's just a matter of how much they can get you to buy in to. Again, every advisor that doesn't charge a fee isn't that way, but many are.

2. Watch your 401(k) investment advisors.

I have worked with employees of large companies as well as employees of large school systems [403(b)]. I have found that many of the assigned representatives don't provide a high level of expertise. Basically, when a new fund comes out that fits a certain investor profile, the sales cycle begins, and they are required to convince clients to add the product to their investment portfolio – without any regard for the long-term consequences.

3. Watch out for tips from friends and family members.
    a. If the financial information or hot stock tip you hear about sounds too good to be true, it is just that... too good to be true. Odds are unlikely that you and your circle of friends and family are the only special people privileged enough to get access to this once-a-lifetime opportunity.
    b. I am not saying that you should never rely on friends or

family, but make sure they are competent and that you treat them just like anyone else when it comes to your money. I have observed several common denominators that undermined the financial planning process:

i. Planners wearing "shiny suits" try harder to become your friend as opposed to serving as your advisor. At a previous firm, I remember the guy with the shiny suit never reading, learning, or advancing his knowledge base. Instead, he spent all his time sending gifts and trying to be a great friend to his clients – at the same time overcharging them and not being competent, ultimately putting their financial futures at risk.

ii. I have seen family members work with their family only because they were family. Not only do you have to work harder to make sure you aren't making an emotional decision, you also have to realize that it is going to be difficult (if not impossible) to fire him or her because you have to see them at each family function. I remember a fellow advisor who worked at the big financial services firm with me never spending time or giving much attention to his largest clients because they were his uncle and aunt. They were affluent and had sophisticated needs which normally required quarterly meetings. He never bothered to make them a priority because he knew they would not fire him, so he could focus on finding new clients. If he was anyone else, they probably would have fired him a long time ago, but because he was family, they could not leave him without breeding familial hostility and creating more problems.

iii. The same is true for using other unqualified relatives or even fellow neighbors or church members – just for the sake of relationship. For years, I watched a particular church make no financial gains on their investments for more than 10 years because a church member who was an insurance agent had been pegged to manage the church's investment portfolio. After years of failed strategy and lackluster performance, I was finally called in to fix the situation. Church leaders shared that the individual should have been fired years earlier, but hadn't been because he was a faithful member of the congregation. That's not to say there aren't qualified, licensed professionals within the church, it is just a warning to make sure you hire the right people for the right reasons – to get the results you want.

**Words of Wisdom**

[Sy] It is difficult to think about wise counsel without considering King Solomon of the Bible. His entire life was a demonstration of the results and consequences of wise counsel or (in some instances) the lack thereof. In his defining moment in 1 Kings 3:9, Solomon sought wisdom from God rather than riches, long life, and vengeance upon his enemies. And as a result of this, God was pleased and blessed him immeasurably with wisdom as well as the wealth that he did not initially ask for.

To pray for wisdom in itself is wise. Was Solomon born with an extraordinary dose of wisdom that the rest of us seem to lack? Yes and No. Certainly the Lord is able to give wisdom from the womb, but no, Solomon proved that he was like any other fallible and flawed person when he went against the ways of the Lord and ultimately paid a price for doing so. But what was the source of Solomon's wisdom? The answer lies in 1 Kings 2:2-4 (ESV). Solomon's wise counsel was delivered through his father, King David. Look at his advisement: "I am about to go the way of all the earth," he said. "So be strong, show yourself a man, and observe what the LORD your God requires: Walk in his ways, and keep his decrees and commands, his laws and requirements, as written in the Law of Moses, so that you may prosper in all you do and wherever you go, and that the LORD may keep his promise to me: 'If your descendants watch how they live, and if they walk faithfully before me with all their heart and soul, you will never fail to have a man on the throne of Israel.'" Wow!

It is easy to miss where the wise seed to pray for wisdom came from.

I would venture to say that Solomon's wisest decision was listening to his Financial Shepherd, who happened to be his father. It is human nature for us to look at where a person is now, especially those of prominent wealth, and not know that there were some decisions along the way that put them in their position. Even those who appear to have been born with a "silver spoon" in their mouth make decisions that could turn that spoon to plastic or platinum. Seeking wise counsel is one of the first crucial steps to becoming a Financial Shepherd. Just as shepherds of old used a staff to guide the sheep under their responsibility and to protect the sheep from potentially hazardous situations, so then the Financial Shepherd's "staff" is the comprehensive financial plan that we will talk about in detail in the upcoming chapters.

Part of being a Financial Shepherd is recognizing that we are not perfect and we do not have all the answers for everything. In fact, true wisdom is to know that on our own accord, we have certain limitations. When we have this awareness, then we can reach out to others that are proficient in the areas where we lack. This holds true in every area of our lives.

For example, when I have car trouble, I contact a mechanic because I have limited experience in this area. Sure, I can do the basics like change the oil or rotate the tires, but when it comes to installing a new fuel tank or replacing the master cylinder, I have to defer to the experts. Furthermore, it is worth my investment to find someone that is knowledgeable and able to provide the best services that will not cost me even more in the long term. At the same time, the life of the vehicle is prolonged.

Consulting wise counsel in regard to your finances is similar to contacting the mechanic for your automobile. There are certain areas of financial planning where you may not be as proficient as the experts. If you take advantage of the best services available to you, then like your vehicle, your long-term financial outlook is brighter.

As counselors, coaches, and co-authors of this book, it is fair to say that we both became Financial Shepherds the hard way - learning a lot of hard lessons along the path from our own lives and from the experiences of our family, friends, and clients. We have made our share of poor decisions that have gone against the wise counsel we know to be vital for every aspect of life. Over the years, we've learned from those mistakes and put those lessons into practice and successful application that we can now share with others.

Proverbs 13:20 (KJV) states, "He that walketh with wise men shall be wise: but a companion of fools shall be destroyed." Proverbs is one of the books of wisdom, so it's only right that we reflect on a verse from this book as it relates to wise counsel. As mentioned previously, it is impossible for us to know everything. In fact God created us in such a way that we are dependent on one another for access to the gifts that he has blessed each one of us with. That said, wisdom suggests that we learn from other people's experiences; their triumphs and tribulations. Wisdom also suggests that we share our experiences so that other people can learn from them and so that we may grow as well. It is necessary for us to keep company *(walketh with)* wise people rather than those *(fools)* who do not have our best interest at heart. We can see this in the "shiny suit guy." He knows how to say all of the right things and he even looks the part. But when you compare him to the authentic Financial Shepherd, the differences are astounding. You begin to recognize the intruder as a wolf in sheep's clothing. But there are ways that you can tell the difference. Look at what he produces and consider the fruit he bears. Of course, the Lord relayed this message much more eloquently in Matthew 7:16-20 (NIV):

*"By their fruit you will recognize them. Do people pick grapes from thornbushes, or figs from thistles? [17]Likewise every good tree bears good fruit, but a bad tree bears bad fruit. [18]A good tree cannot bear bad fruit, and a bad tree cannot bear good fruit. [19]Every tree that does not bear good fruit is cut down and thrown into the fire. [20]Thus, by their fruit you will recognize them"* (Matthew 7:16- 20).

The Chief Financial Shepherd said it best. The example He used was in regard to false prophets, but the same holds true for anyone pretending to be something that they are not. You will be able to tell who they are by the fruit they bear. The wise counselor is no exception. His references are often substantiated by the exemplary life that he lives. In regard to financial planning, those that have benefited from his advice will not only tell you, but the results will speak for themselves. And most importantly, He will acknowledge that he is nothing apart from God, the provider and source of all true wisdom and wise counsel.

Rejecting wise counsel can have devastating consequences. Consider what happened to the infrastructure of America's financial and banking systems when the long-held financial protections in place were removed:

*Reversal of the Glass-Steagall Act:* Although we've all been impacted by it, most Americans are unfamiliar with the Glass-Steagall Act, also known as The Banking Act of 1933, which established the Federal Deposit Insurance Corporation (FDIC), offering consumer protection measures for banking customers. The legislation was repealed in 1999, effectively removing the separation that previously existed between Wall Street investment banks and depository banks, allowing all banks, insurance companies, and investment firms to sell the same financial products with little to no regulation. That is the reason today why several of these firms (i.e., AIG) are considered "too big to fail." The resulting collapse of these corporations would cripple the U.S. economy because of the far-reaching financial implications and involvement of the firms in all segments of the market. The problem is that many of the so-called financial experts didn't have the right expertise to enter into each others' worlds and guess who paid the price? Not them, WE DID! We had to bail them out, and in the process it became more difficult for consumers to borrow money or access credit. Now we have lower savings rates (like CD interest rates), many lost jobs, record unemployment, a failing housing market, and the greatest economic downturn since the Great Depression of the 1930s. Selfishness, corruption and greed fueled the financial fire that decimated retirement accounts, pension funds, savings accounts, investment portfolios, and the stock market; shaking the very core of our national economy.

The time has arrived for us to return to the wisdom of our forefathers and rely on the strength of their experience and expertise. Without question, there is a need for spiritual repentance and reflection to acknowledge our downfall and return to the way of righteousness.

*"The fear of the Lord is the beginning of wisdom, and knowledge of the Holy One is understanding" (Proverbs 9:10 NIV). "If you are wise, your wisdom will reward you" (Proverbs 9:12a NIV).*

# Chapter 5 – The Warning Signs of Financial Failure

"Failure is not a single, cataclysmic event. You don't fail overnight. Instead, failure is a few errors in judgment, repeated every day." ~Jim Rohn

[Sy] As with any type of failure, it is very difficult to point the finger at one particular cause. When I meet with couples after years of frustration in their marriage, there is never just one thing that caused the marriage to spiral downward – and ultimately out of control. After a long season of college basketball, there is never just one thing that caused the team not to win a national championship. Most likely, there was a series of errors; missed shots, poor passes, turnovers, and missed opportunities adding up to a loss.

Likewise, if you are on the brink of financial failure, there is not just one thing that you can identify to be the root cause of your circumstances. There are probably several things including poor financial habits and training, inadequate financial knowledge, reckless spending habits, bad debts, mismanagement of credit, etc. Although there are many things that lead to financial failure, there is some commonality in each scenario. If there was ever a simple answer to the cause of failure in general, it would have to be poor financial planning and lack of preparation. Perhaps the best skill set to hone is that of preparation and planning because it can affect the outcome of every aspect of our lives. Preparation and planning do not require any type of educational degree, but they do require effort. They are not necessarily spiritual gifts, yet they do require wisdom. Careful execution can create the subtle difference between being rich and being wealthy. Christ also placed emphasis on the importance of planning. In Luke 14:28- 30 (NIV), His example transcends the barriers of time.

*The Financial Shepherd*

The passage reads, *"Suppose one of you wants to build a tower. Will he not first sit down and estimate the cost to see if he has enough money to complete it? For if he lays the foundation and is not able to finish it, everyone who sees it will ridicule him, saying, 'This fellow began to build and was not able to finish...'"*

Isn't this what happens when we fail to plan? When viewed from God's perspective, the lack of planning seems to be quite careless, let alone costly. Later on, we will talk about the importance of setting goals as this is the all-important start to preparation and planning.

[Glen] Years ago there was a couple referred to the firm for financial counseling because they were behind on every bill. They were paying the minimum on credit cards that were all but maxed out, yet still finding a way to keep living their same lifestyle. Their mother had helped them for years and then she died. The mother did not have much life insurance, so they were now on their own. The couple did not budget or do any advance financial planning. They didn't get serious at all until their car was repossessed, and that's when they asked for help. In their situation, losing the car was the best thing for them because they needed a wakeup call. The wife could no longer afford to shop at Neiman Marcus, nor could he have season tickets to watch NBA games anymore. These were educated people with great careers who on the outside appeared to have no problems at all. But in reality, they had all the warning signs of financial failure.

It is difficult to open up about money, especially when you are hurting and especially when you feel obligated to keep up the appearance that everything is perfect. Those same people who are good clients now (after getting their finances straightened out), lied to me initially in our first meeting because they were ashamed of how bad things had gotten. However, one thing is always true, the numbers never lie. As we got more and more involved, they opened up, and our team was able to help them. No one can help you as long as you are living a lie. Keeping secrets never works. God sends us vessels to help, but first we have to admit to ourselves that we need help and that we can do better than what we are doing now.

Another example is that of an engaged couple ready to get married, but the woman lied about about her amount of credit card debt. After they were married the truth came out due to her terrible spending habits, and it nearly broke them up. It took time, but she finally followed a budget and stopped her elaborate spending, and now all is well. You can save a lot of time and energy by being truthful in the beginning because lies will always come out in the end.

As the saying goes, 'Robbing Peter to pay Paul' is a common warning sign of impending financial doom, and it will always catch up to you. However, it can make sense for emergencies if you borrow money at a low- to no-interest rate in order to pay off a high-interest item. Not only do you pay less in interest, your payment amount also goes down. However, what I have found is that many people only pay the lower payment, and have to transfer the payment again and normally there are even higher fees associated with that. In addition, there is a sense of relief because the financial burden has been lifted, and many people revert back to their old spending habits. That is a dangerous game to play, and it usually backfires. When you identify a financial warning sign, the best thing to do is seek assistance and change the path you're going down immediately.

Too-good-to-be-true refinancing deals are rarely as good as you think they are. It is never a good idea to refinance any depreciable asset like a car unless there is a dramatic difference in interest rate. Never take out more money, because now you are paying longer on something that has even less value. There is something called *liquidity*, and you always want to try and owe less than what the asset is worth. Emergencies happen, and the more *liquid* you are, the better you can recover from the perils of life.

Frequently running out of money before running out of month is a common warning sign. This situation typically means you pay the minimum amount due on bills, you have rolling credit card balances, and your check is spent as soon as it comes in. This is no way to live. This scenario means you are simply overextended. There are changes that have to be made in the budget, sacrifices like eating out less, turning off unnecessary expenses such as digital or cable television, and shopping less. These things aren't necessarily easy to do, but if you follow a strict budget, you may be able to escape a bad situation before it gets worse.

## [Sy] "The Top 5 Irrational Thoughts About Money"

*If you share some of these common thoughts about money, consider them to be Financial Warning Signs on a path headed toward disaster, and start altering your course now!*

1. **More money is the answer to every problem**

   Many people from different walks of life and across different economic and social strata would readily agree with this statement. However, if you happen to gain access to more money but you haven't learned the appropriate tools of managing the money, then in due time your problems will continue and quite possibly be amplified. Having more money without the right mindset is like purchasing the shell of a 2011 BMW 7 Series and trying to make it work on the engine and chassis of a 1990 Oldsmobile Cutlass. Pretty soon, the differences will be quite obvious because the same problems that you were having out of that Cutlass prior to its makeover, will eventually take its toll.

   For all intents and purposes, the bottom line is if you aren't good with managing $10, you will not appropriately manage $10,000 - and will most likely find it even more difficult to handle. In fact, having more money brings new challenges and responsibilities. For instance, you may have been able to handle your own taxes when you were making $75,000, but now that you're making $275,000 there are many more things to consider, and if you don't know what you're doing it could cause severe problems and cost in significant penalties. Having more money usually isn't the solution to a financial problem, instead it is effectively managing the money you already have and following God's financial plan.

2. **God wants all Christians to be rich (e.g., 'Prosperity Gospel')**

   A popular motivational speaker recently said during a presentation that, "Money doesn't make you happy, but everyone wants to find out for themselves." However true that might be, it's important to remember that true wealth is not just measured in dollars and cents. Remember: Dollars + Change = Sense. There are so many more things to life than money (health, love, family, hobbies, etc). However it often takes money to accomplish and experience many of the abundant fruits of life. God does want you to be successful, but He does not want that success to bankrupt your soul.

The recent popularity of the so-called Prosperity Gospel movement has single-handedly misled hundreds of thousands, potentially millions of people into falsely believing that God's will for all Christians is super-wealth and riches. This simply isn't true. The Bible clearly states that there will always be poor people. And numerous parables illustrate that individuals and families are given varying levels of talents and wealth to manage; not all are equally rich with material wealth. It is clear that the Prosperity movement has only enriched a few people; however, it has misguided millions more by focusing too much on the gifts rather than the Giver. It is vital that each of us knows what the Word of God says, because ultimately we will be held accountable for what we say and do.

Certainly God is able to make all Christians rich if that is His will; because Luke 1: 37 tells us 'for nothing shall be impossible with God.' The question must be then, is it God's will for all Christians to be rich? The answer is that Christians have access to God's wealth, but wealth isn't solely measured in money and possessions. We have many examples throughout the Bible, like the young, rich man whom Christ challenged to leave everything to gain eternal life. What about the parable of the poor widow who gave above (percentage-wise) the others who were rich? 2 Corinthians 9:10-11 (NIV) states, "Now he who supplies seed to the sower and bread for food will also supply and increase your store of seed and will enlarge the harvest of your righteousness. You will be made rich in every way so that you can be generous on every occasion, and through us your generosity will result in thanksgiving to God." According to verses 10 and 11, the result is not always financial abundance but even better; righteousness and favor with God. One important thing to remember is that God is the author and finisher of all things, and He does not owe anyone anything. We should be grateful for any and all blessings that we have.

### 3. **Poverty is a form of godliness**

Poverty has nothing to do with godliness. God does not want to see His people broke, busted, and disgusted. However, He also does not want us to worship money or material idols by making them a priority instead of Him. Many consider those that live in poverty to be meek and humble because they don't have any material possessions that interfere with worshiping God. This is quite the contrary. Living in a state of poverty can actually be the opposite of godliness because our focus shifts from worshipping and serving God to struggling for survival to make ends meet. Throughout history, there have been numerous individuals that have taken a vow of poverty to focus on the things of God; however, these people are usually living in self-contained communities where the need for money is practically non-existent. Also, their basic needs are provided for by sponsoring ministries or organizations, and they have adequate land and resources to grow crops and provide daily sustenance. Most people do not have access to such communities with extra land for gardening or raising livestock, so they must work and make money to acquire basic necessities. Most people are not called to live in poverty. In our society, many are impoverished as a result or consequence of societal inequities and financial mismanagement – not a higher calling from God.

4. **It's not polite or appropriate to discuss money**

It's often said that any problem you cannot talk about, you most likely cannot solve. I have often wondered where this 'money taboo' derived. For so long, money has been considered the ultimate measuring stick, essentially, a way to keep score. Maybe it is because so many divisive schemes have evolved around getting more money. One thing is for sure, money definitely demands attention when it is the topic of conversation. Unfortunately, most people are not comfortable talking about money. In fact, they would rather talk about their deepest, darkest personal secrets rather than divulge their annual salary to someone else. This lack of communication transfers over into relationships and marriages and has the potential to sever the strongest relationships.

In pre-marital sessions, I challenge this behavior by asking, 'What do you hide from your fiancé?' About 90 percent of respondents will answer "nothing." I follow up with other questions: 'Have you told them about your previous partners?' About 85 percent will answer "yes." 'Does your fiancé/fiancée know how much income you bring home with each paycheck?' 'Do they know how much you have in your checking and savings accounts?' 'Do they know how much debt you currently have?' 'Do they know about your credit?' The number of people answering "yes" to these questions is overwhelmingly small. Not only is it appropriate to communicate about money, it is absolutely necessary.

5. **Children shouldn't be involved in family financial discussions**

Training and teaching children how to become Financial Shepherds starts before they know anything about money. It begins with the toys and the belongings that parents provide for them. As parents, we should teach our children to take care of the things that belong to others even better than their own things. Notice this change from the typical mindset of our society.

Since everything belongs to God, we teach our children "everything belongs to God": the house, cars, money, everything! Since this is the case, we are to take care of God's possessions better than our own. Children are more impressionable, so this will sink in sooner than you realize. In fact, my 5-year-old daughter finds joy in saying, "Daddy, this is God's house." If she understands that lesson at age 5, imagine how far ahead of the financial game she will be when she's older and responsible for her own finances. The most important way to teach this principle to children is for parents to live it daily. When you change the way you think about finances, those that depend on you and follow your lead, will also have a changed mindset.

Don't be afraid to talk to your children even if you aren't where you want to be financially. Make it a point to tell your children the truth (age-appropriate information that they can comprehend). Even if you are in a bad place, give them a basic sense of your family's financial reality so they don't live in fairytale land and have unreasonable expectations. This level of honesty will prevent your children from making the same mistakes you made. On the flip side, if you are financially stable or well-to-do, inform your children of that as well. Focus on the fact that God has blessed your family with more resources so that they will demonstrate the principle of 'blessed to be a blessing.' The point is to be honest with your children and prepare them to be good stewards and future Financial Shepherds.

> **$$$** When you change the way you think about finances, those that depend on you and follow your lead, will also have a changed mindset.

# Chapter 6 – Is the Mirror Broken, Or Am I?

If you've ever been in a Fun House at a carnival or a fair, then you know how different you can look depending upon the mirror that you're looking in. There are mirrors that can make you look 10 feet tall, or five feet wide. There are mirrors that contort your shape and proportions to the extent that you can hardly recognize your own reflection. On first glance, you know it's you because you're standing there and can recognize the clothes or shoes you have on, but everything else is so different, it is difficult to tell what's real. In the Fun House, how you look in the mirror is not necessarily how you look in real life. The good news about these mirrors is that they are for entertainment purposes only - just for fun. The bad news is that some of us need to take a second look - because the distorted images we see reflected aren't that far from the truth.

*Are you broken, or is the mirror you're holding broken?* There's a childhood superstition about broken mirrors that says whoever breaks a mirror will have seven years of bad luck. The problem with superstition is that is requires an individual to rely on luck and circumstances instead of trusting in God and His word. Regardless of whether you broke the mirror, or just looked into a cracked mirror and saw a broken reflection, the real question is what are you going to do about what you see looking back at you? In life, the broken mirror is mostly about the tools and habits that are used to help build or destroy our lives (i.e., poor financial planning, excessive spending habits, etc.). But a broken or cracked mirror also can represent an opportunity to start anew; to gain a fresh start and launch a new attempt to do things differently. Owning up to our flaws and broken way of thinking opens the door for improvement and gives us a chance to let God make us into who He created us to be - instead of what the world sees and expects us to be.

The broken person or broken "man in the mirror" has more to do with how a person thinks and how their decisions have produced the consequences they are now facing in life. Brokenness is a mindset that needs to be changed from the inside out because it affects every other area of life. True brokenness is an emotional state that requires healing from a spiritual and emotional perspective. You can usually spot broken people hiding behind their money and material possessions trying to mask the fact that they are hurting. Many once-famous athletes, entertainers, and celebrities who have lost their wealth by squandering away millions fall into the category of brokenness. All the money, fame, influence, and fortunes in the world still are not enough to bandage those wounds or erase the mental and emotional scars they carry. Whether it's the mirror or the person that's broken, taking a good look at yourself and making a commitment to change is the first step.

There's a great quote by Mahatma Gandhi that says, "Be the change you want to see in the world." We submit to you that real change only comes when you allow God to change you too. And the only way to truly accept change in yourself is to know exactly what you're dealing with by taking a good, long look in the mirror. The majority of people we've counseled over the years are living a double life. We're not talking about a secret agent, hidden agenda, and clandestine type of life. We're talking about something less sinister, but equally as damaging because they are living lives they cannot afford built on lies they cannot sustain. Most people live the life they want other people to see, and then build a reputation on it. Then there's the life representative of who they really are. In most instances, those lives are vastly different, and the common denominator is money.

Something we have learned about money over the years is that it tells the truth about who a person is. If you follow the money trail, you can learn almost anything and everything about someone that you need to know to better understand who they are, where they're going, what they want out of life, and what their plan is to accomplish it.

On the outside, many people live like their finances are under control and they have all the money they need to fund the extravagant and luxurious lifestyles they lead. However, on the inside, many of the people who have come to us for help are financially barren - practically destitute

- and can barely afford the designer clothes on their backs, much less the luxury automobiles and huge houses they live in.

How you spend your money is often a good gauge of where you are in your life. Something we say in our business is, "Follow the money." When you identify where someone spends most of their time and money, you can learn a lot about them and find out what their priorities are. For some, it's a matter of basic necessities like keeping the lights on and putting food on the table. For others, it's a matter of appearances such as frequent trips to the hair and nail salons and sporting the latest designer bag and shoes - regardless of the fact that most of these expenditures are paid on credit and almost never paid off in full. For most, it's keeping up appearances - and living up to the professional degrees, titles, and positions that have been acquired. It is often about joining the right country club, paying for private school, living in certain neighborhoods, dining at certain restaurants, and basically bankrolling the present while bankrupting the future.

The need to "perform" for others by pretending to be something we're not indicates a level of hurt, insecurity, and brokenness that has yet to be healed. Brokenness highlights our flaws and our vulnerabilities - something no one really wants to admit they have. Yet it is during these moments of deep reflection and humility that we are able to admit that we need help and are unable to do it alone. In reality, we all experience a state of brokenness at some point in our lives. For some it may be financial turmoil, for others a broken heart after investing many years into a marriage that still ends in divorce. Others come from a place of brokenness brought on by a dysfunctional family or home life, while others fall prey to addiction or victimization. Regardless of the path traveled, most people end up in the same place of brokenness and end up struggling to survive in a situation that is totally out of control. Most of these people, whether they admit it or not, are desperately searching for someone to help them mend and find a true sense of self.

The unfortunate thing about desperation and despair is sometimes it takes hitting rock bottom before we ever seek out assistance or decide to change. Some of us simply have to be broken before we can be restored. The good news is that God is in the restoration business - specializing in healing the brokenhearted and repairing the breaches in our lives. When we are broke or broken, we are weak. But it is in our weakness that God's strength is made perfect. In our fallen state, His sufficient grace rebuilds and restores our strength and our faith and trust in Him. To be clear, although it is not God's will that we incur debt or live in financial ruin, it is His will that we rely on Him completely to provide for our needs, wants, and desires.

A beautiful passage of scripture can be found in Romans 5:3-4 (ESV) "…we rejoice in our sufferings, knowing that suffering produces endurance, and endurance produces character, and character produces hope." Despite the problems we face, it is reassuring to know that "this too shall pass." Even when the final collection notices arrive, and bill collectors are trying to reach you at home, at work, at your mother's house, and on your cell phone, it's comforting to know that during these difficult moments, we can still put our trust in God and rely on Him to bring us through - better and stronger than before.

**Doctrine of Debt vs. Financial Leverage**

Ironically, although America was built on Christian principles of godly order, our society reinforces recklessness and irresponsibility with money which is a contradiction to what the Bible requires from believers. In general, we spend too much, we don't save enough, we are too emotionally attached to money, and we don't teach basic financial stewardship and pass on financial wisdom to our children so they can learn to make better financial decisions for the future. Just glance at any newspaper or financial magazine headline, and they all say pretty much the same thing: That the U.S. economy is struggling to survive and that it is buried alive under the weight of government and consumer debt. Individuals are in debt, families are in debt, businesses are in debt, non-profits are in debt, churches are in debt, states are in the debt, the country is in debt; the whole world is in debt.

If debt is such a bad thing, then why does everything around us seem to say it's OK? God's truth is that it is not OK. Unfortunately, the majority of us have fallen into the trap of chasing wants instead of securing needs and we have unnecessarily created a pile of debt that we cannot manage or repay in a timely fashion.

What is debt? It is something that is owed, or the state of being in which you owe something that must be repaid. Although you can turn on any financial or business news station and hear the terms "good debt" and "bad debt" being tossed around, this understanding of debt is a contradiction of God's will for His people. The business world determines good debt by its ability to expand financial leverage, build a credit payment history, and the company's ability to repay the debt. Bad debt is determined to be a debt load (accumulated debt and debt-to-income ratios) for which the company or organization is unlikely to be able to meet its financial obligations, hence putting investors and creditors at risk of not getting reimbursed for loans or investments made to finance the business. Either way you look at it, debt puts the debtor at a disadvantage.

Debt dishonors God and contradicts His word. There is nothing in the Word of God that supports financial irresponsibility. Quite the contrary, we are instructed to work, budget (count the costs), and invest our talents and treasures into opportunities that yield a good harvest in their returns. We are admonished in Proverbs 22:7 that no matter how much money we have, the process of getting into debt dictates that the borrower will always be servant/slave to the lender. Yes, the Bible acknowledges that money is a needed resource in our society, but it also instructs us to keep our priorities straight by avoiding a "love of money" which is the root of all evil, and by making sure our values are focused on spiritual and eternal treasures that don't corrupt, corrode, or fade away.

**Financial Leveraging** is the responsible and acceptable use of credit or external financial resources to gain or increase the value of wealth. Financial Leveraging is not borrowing beyond the ability to pay back, and it is not shifting money from one source to another to cover basic expenses. Financial Leveraging is a tool and process that creates access to opportunities for investment and financial growth. We should remove the philosophy of debt from our vocabularies and focus on our ability to use financial leveraging to our advantage.

During our counseling sessions, we're sometimes asked the question, 'Is there a difference between being broke and being poor?' Although nobody wants to be in either situation, it is crucial to understand that the distinctions and the necessary steps to change the circumstances for each one are different. In general, there are three categories where you find persistent financial struggle and turmoil: broke, working poor and impoverished.

A lot of people are broke. Not because they don't make enough money, but because they spend too much money on things that don't have real value. People who are broke often find themselves "robbing Peter to pay Paul" because they just couldn't pass up the opportunity to purchase some material item that does little or nothing to build wealth. Broke people can make a little money or a lot of money, but the thing they have in common is that they don't have a plan to not be broke. To quote one of our colleagues, "If you don't know where you're going, how will you know when you get there?" People who are broke tend to wander any path in search of a way out. The problem is they don't know where the way out leads to, so they end up aimlessly wandering, repeating the same financial mistakes day after day, week after week, month after month, year after year. Making more money does not solve the problem because they do not have a financial goal to meet or a financial plan to follow. Broke people are infamous for trying to spend their way out of debt; a paradoxical process that is destined to fail because it defies the laws of finance and simply doesn't make sense.

It would be astonishing to a lot of broke people to find out how much money they actually have earned and blown over the years with absolutely nothing to show for it. They've spent thousands of dollars on clothes, cars, dining, entertainment, rent, gambling, lottery tickets, and "sure-fire, get-rich-quick schemes" that gave them nothing but false hope. Had those poor purchasing decisions been avoided, and those dollars been invested instead, there's a great possibility they wouldn't still be in the broke category, but would be well on their way to financial freedom.

The working poor fall into a bit of a precarious situation, in that they tend not to waste a lot of money, but they are forced into making tough choices about what is or is not necessary or affordable. For example, a husband who falls into the working poor category might be struggling to pay the rent for his family's apartment because the only other places he can afford are undesirable or unsafe to live in. The choice boils down to getting ahead or staying alive. The working poor often are faced with huge financial obstacles with dire consequences that may be unavoidable such as paying for uninsured medical expenses and prescriptions. The options in front of them are to pay basic bills or to remain healthy so they can keep working to pay for a lifestyle that they cannot afford. An article published by Bloomberg Press titled, "U.S. Minimum Wage Doesn't Cover Family Living Costs, Study Says" confirms additional reports and studies stating that since the turn of the 21$^{st}$ century, a family with a fully employed parent and two children cannot afford basic living expenses on a minimum wage income. A cost of living study featuring 10 different areas throughout the nation indicated that earning minimum wage no longer provides enough income to live without additional government assistance through programs like subsidized childcare, health care, and food stamps. The working poor literally cannot afford to live in America.

According to the U.S. Department of Health and Human Services, the 2009 poverty guideline rate for a family of four is $22,050. The U.S. Census Bureau, the U.S. Department of Labor, and the U.S. Department of

Health and Human Services all use statistical data from poverty thresholds and poverty guidelines to determine various income levels that define poverty in different states or regions and to determine which income levels are low enough to meet federal requirements to receive financial assistance. Basically, living in poverty means that an individual's or family's income does not meet the designated poverty guideline or threshold for the cost of living in their area. In America, living in poverty is the equivalent of digging a ditch while you're standing in it - with the likelihood of getting out rapidly decreasing as time passes because the hole only gets deeper.

People who are impoverished think differently from people who are broke. A poverty mentality is essentially a defeated mentality because there is no apparent way out of the situation. Poverty is a state of being and a state of mind in which the individuals who are entrapped cannot see a way out or identify and access relevant tools, skills, or resources to change their circumstances. Usually, when someone is living in poverty, everyone around them is in poverty too. And when all you see is poverty, and all you know is poverty, there is no incentive to dream or aspire to anything different or better, because there isn't anyone around to teach you how to get out of poverty. Furthermore, the state of poverty and the government infrastructure to assist those living in poverty actually perpetuates the cycle of impoverishment. When individuals and families are resigned to hopelessness, and it *pays more not to work* than it does to work, the system fosters a sense of dependency and reliance upon others to get what is wanted or needed. Instead of pursuing a helping-hand, individuals with a poverty mentality prefer a handout because that is what they have become accustomed to. Instead of following the Biblical principles of working, tithing, saving, investing, sowing, and giving, there's a pattern of idling in inactivity with the expectation that someone else will foot the bill through programs and services and subsidized assistance. There is no inclination to change because the financial assistance provided is easily lost or taken away if the aforementioned poverty threshold is approached. So, for those who would desire to be out of poverty, there is no incentive to work their way out of it, because our federal "welfare state" and system of dependence and co-dependence on the government has been institutionally reinforced. As a nation, we need to collectively change how we talk, act, educate, and think about money to prepare future generations for financial survival.

## What Are You Thinking?

A principle paradigm shift for successful living in the 21st century requires a change of mind about money and a sincere effort to shift our focus to God. We have mistakenly fallen into the trap of hedonistic, self-reliance and convinced ourselves that we are masters of our own destiny and fate. To some degree, yes, we must take personal responsibility for our actions and decisions; however, we must not fail to incorporate our accountability to God. It is a dangerous path to traverse that doesn't include God on the journey.

Our financial goals should not conclude simply at getting rich, but rather, they should also incorporate building wealth. Although there are a lot of rich people in the world, many of them are not wealthy because they cannot sustain their riches. Wealth is like an evergreen tree that always remains the same regardless of the season. Think about what an evergreen looks like. It has full, green, plush leaves or spines even if it is surrounded by bees buzzing in the spring in search of pollen, or drenched from a late summer shower, or swayed by a mid-autumn breeze, or weighed down by a late winter's snowfall. Underneath whatever else is going on, is still that same healthy, stable, viable tree. Much like wealth, evergreens are unburdened by external circumstances and the environment because their roots run much deeper than the temporary situations around them.

We should aspire to build wealth because it brings peace of mind by allowing an individual to focus on future goals instead of being consumed by the day-to-day ups and downs of their finances. Most wealthy people live well below the means of what they can actually afford - mainly because they understand the true value of money; what it is, what it isn't, and what matters most.

One of the best lessons you can learn about money is this: When you change your mind, you can change your destiny. 'As a man thinketh, so is he' (Proverbs 23:7 KJV). What are you thinking about?

Christians are called to be leaders, not followers of the world's flawed economic system. But the reality is that if you're broke, nobody cares what you have to say. Too many intelligent, anointed, and talented Christian voices are suppressed or ignored because they have no stake in the financial game - so therefore no one takes them seriously. People gravitate and listen to people who are deemed successful, and unfortunately that success is often defined by the world in terms of dollars and cents. To become true ambassadors for God, we need to get our spiritual and financial houses in order so that we can be an example for others to follow. In business, one must pay to play, and if you cannot afford to get in the game, there is little chance that your voice will be heard.

An important first step in accomplishing financial independence is recognition of our own limitations. A key next step is identifying and addressing the mentality behind debt accumulation and then dissecting the underlying issues that motivate those spending decisions. A Financial Shepherd plays a crucial role in the process of ensuring that you have the necessary knowledge and resources to correctly address and adjust your financial situation.

> **$$$** When you are willing to change your mind, you automatically obtain the power to change your destiny.

# Chapter 7 – The Battle for Financial Freedom

[Sy]    I think it is safe to say that most people aren't familiar with the term "generational curse." But for those who have been oppressed for years, decades, or centuries by the same negative patterns of behavior that are consistent within a family—or a culture—then generational curses are quite familiar. Bad habits, addictions, debt, poverty, circumstances, lifestyle, and life philosophies are passed from one generation to another without correction, and often to the detriment of hundreds of unsuspecting family member victims. Recognizing and altering these behaviors is a vital component of the *Change* needed in the Dollars + Change = Sense equation.

Many 12-step programs for addiction often assert that the first step to overcoming a problem or addictive behavior is admitting that there actually is a problem. The same is true in overcoming financial addictions and poor spending habits - often created as a result of unbroken generational curses. In order to break a generational curse, you must first admit there is a problem. That problem might be overspending, debt, poor cash management, living above your means, or lack of financial prowess and the ability to do responsible financial planning. Rarely is the problem just not making enough money. The sad reality is that if the majority of broke people made more money, they would spend more money and still be in the same predicament. So the answer is found not in making more, but in being a better steward of what you already have.

My mother was 15 years old when she had me. She was a single mother also raised by a single mother. We lived in a tough neighborhood - one of the poorest communities in Memphis, Tennessee. To be honest, we didn't have a lot of money, and the money that we did have was usually squandered - or not used in a profitable or beneficial way. Looking back, I believe that my mother and I grew up together, raised by her mom - my grandmother - who taught us to make change through hard work and personal responsibility. We learned to have a good work ethic, but not how to effectively manage money. I believe that she didn't teach us a lot about money because she didn't have a lot of knowledge about money. The bottom line is that you cannot teach what you do not know.

As a young adult, I realized that I too had been the victim of a financial generational curse. Unbeknownst to me, a debt mentality and pattern of living beyond my means had been passed down for years through various members of my family who perpetuated a cycle of poverty. Repeatedly I would spend my last dime, and then borrow a nickel, to purchase something I wanted, but couldn't afford. That way of thinking was all I knew. But here's what I learned: the key to conquering financial strongholds is to admit that there's a problem, accept that you don't have all the answers, and change your mind about remaining a victim. Conquerors are not victims, they are victors. I realize now that my upbringing and lack of financial guidance is a major part of the reason I'm a therapist now. Like so many others, I too was lost, but was blessed to realize the error of my ways – and then made a decision to change.

To break the generational curse of poverty or financial failure requires introducing new techniques and tools into the financial equation. Our entire family had a poverty mentality, so no one in our small, tight-knit group could uplift anyone else. In my years as a counselor, one of the things I came to realize was that a lot of people want to change, but simply don't know how. They don't know how to start, they don't know where to start, and they don't know who to trust.

## Pathway to Financial Freedom

If you want to change your entire life for the better, you must first change the way you think about money. Money isn't everything, money isn't the key to happiness, but money is a necessary resource in our society. Having a working knowledge about money and its benefits or pitfalls can be the difference between poverty or wealth, success or failure, life and death.

The first step on the path to financial freedom is to acknowledge that God is in control. None of the money we make or the things we have belong to us; they all belong to Him. We are simply stewards or overseers of His resources. It is imperative that we focus on the divine financial plan for our lives, and not be misled by society's failing financial systems. We are called to be financial leaders and Financial Shepherds. We are not called to duplicate the destructive and poor financial habits we see around us. When we accept that God owns it all and our spiritual obligation is to fulfill His Will according to His Word, then knowing what our financial priorities are becomes much easier. This new way of thinking allows you to break free from the self-imposed limitations of your own ability and open your mind to God's unlimited possibilities. Since all things are possible through Christ, there is no limit on when and how the windows of heaven may open to pour out blessings upon you.

One of the lessons we teach throughout this book is to think about money as an extension of God's ministry for us here on earth. Instead of viewing money as a must-have commodity, we encourage people to view it as one of many other resources to accomplish the will of God. When we release ownership and emotional attachments to money and how we view it, using it correctly and responsibly becomes second nature.

The next step to overcoming failure in finances and being a good financial steward is understanding that choices have consequences. When looking at the past, present, and future, we must realize and accept that the only thing we can control or change is the "here and now." We are in a present state of being because of what we did in the past. And even though we cannot change the past, we can glance back over our shoulder to learn from past experiences (good or bad) and then adjust our behavior to make different or better decisions in the future. Even though we can't predict or dictate future occurrences, we can make decisions that will positively affect our future results.

Every financial choice you make (or have made) has a specific consequence attached to it. For example, when an entry-level employee chooses to spend his or her paycheck on shoes and a new outfit instead of household bills, the resulting consequence is much greater than just the money spent on clothes and shoes. Although the material value of the items might be $250, the perceived value of loss is much greater. In addition to the replacement funds that must cover the bills, there are also the added costs of late fees and penalties for not paying bills on time, the immeasurable loss of trust because the individual was irresponsible in spending, and the intangible expense of time loss and extra work that has to be done to compensate for the original error in judgment. The added stress created by not making a good decision in the first place can have an adverse effect on future job performance—which may have even greater financial consequences—and also negatively impact one's health due to unnecessary stress. As the saying goes, 'we don't get ulcers by what we eat, but by what's eating us.' Unfortunately, poor financial decisions always cost more than they're worth.

Depending upon how much money you're talking about, some financial choices have long-term consequences that may take years to overcome. For example, I have a client who suffers from major chronic depression. She went through a painful divorce and proceeded to self-medicate through shopping and maxing out her credit cards to make purchases that had previously been denied because of a "very controlling husband" who would not approve such purchases. As a result of her shopping spree, she has since accumulated more than $21,000 in credit card debt in the past year. The truth is that she cannot change or control what has already occurred in her marriage, and she cannot control what additional challenges the future may bring. However, she can learn from her mistakes and choose to make different decisions based on past lessons learned. She can either choose to continue the same destructive path she's currently on, or she can choose to follow a new plan that has been developed and presented to her in order to create the future she desires. Ultimately, the choice is hers. Similarly, the choice is yours.

**Nature Versus Nurture**

Just like in science, the nature versus nurture argument exists in finances. Is good financial stewardship born or learned? Are poor financial decisions automatic or acquired? In reality, it's a bit of both. We are genetically predisposed to mirror characteristics and traits existent in our genes. However, we obtain the majority of our financial prowess - or lack thereof - from our parents or guardians based on what we observe growing up. The downside is that historically, parents have kept money a secret from their children, hence failing to protect them from the devastation of debt, poor credit, and financial mismanagement. Also, by shielding children from the realities of financial decisions, we have inadvertently raised a generation of people ill-equipped and unprepared to make the necessary financial preparations to position themselves to afford and maintain the lifestyles they actually desire.

Money management and proper financial planning should not be kept secret. Money is too much a part of our lives to not openly discuss it and provide a basic foundation of understanding in families, classrooms, and church congregations. There is no limit to the amount of financial destruction that has been caused as a result of secrecy surrounding money. Whether a financial situation is good, bad, or indifferent, the most effective strategy for improving it is an open and frank discussion about money.

For years, Christians in particular have developed a negative connotation about money by going to one extreme or the other. In one camp, people feel that having money or wealth is sinful and hinders your ability to serve God. In the other camp, people feel that you can simply embrace a popular Prosperity Gospel to "name it and claim it" and riches will literally fall out of the sky into the lives of God's chosen people. The truth lies somewhere in the middle. God has no intention for His people to be in lack. As a matter of fact, He has made abundant provision for everything that is needed. However, money can be a problem if it separates an individual from God and His plan and purpose for his life. In all things, seek moderation.

The truth is that God isn't concerned about how much wealth an individual has or doesn't have. He's concerned about financial stewardship - and what that individual does with the resources He provides. Whether someone is tithing on a dollar or a million dollars is irrelevant. If God isn't a priority and if His will isn't the guiding factor, then money will always be a problem and a source of contention throughout life.

When it comes to breaking generational curses, I'm often asked if you can simply 'Pray your way out of debt.' The answer is: "No, not if that's all you're doing." Remember, faith without works is dead. So in order to breathe life back into your financial situation, you have to work, pray, and demonstrate faith in God's promises for provision. You have to change your mind and change the way you think about money. The good news is that you do not have to do it alone.

Sometimes overcoming poor financial habits and breaking the poverty mentality requires changing surroundings and also changing some relationships. Just like birds of a feather flock together, like-minded people tend to hang out together. But once you change your mind about money, you may also have to change some of the relationships around you to accommodate your new financial direction and priorities.

The key types of old relationships to dismantle are those that distract you from your divine purpose and deter you from accomplishing your new financial goals. Relationships with individuals who have a poverty mentality and who constantly drain you emotionally and financially need to be reassessed. Ask yourself three questions to determine what types of relationships to hold on to or let go: 1) Is this person pushing me toward or pulling me away from my divine purpose in life? 2) Is this person pushing me toward or pulling me away from my ultimate financial objective in life? 3) Is this person building me up or tearing me down as it relates to my financial future?

No matter how much money you have, once you commit to following a financial plan, one of the primary new relationships to acquire is that of a reputable banker and/or financial planner. This individual should be a key member of your personal financial resource management team or board of directors. This person should be a trusted advisor who understands and shares your spiritual priorities and goals for your financial well-being. The individual should support your dreams, not belittle them or tear them down.

The goal in establishing these new relationships is to systematically build a new financial support system around you that's constructed of mature, responsible advisors who reflect the values you want to uphold and who know how to get where you want to go. These new relationships are established on the principles of common vision and purpose. This new support system is made of individuals who are on board with your personal financial and wealth management plan, and individuals committed to being honest with you about your spending, saving, and investment habits.

As we begin the process of conquering our finances, it will be important to start thinking through a new financial lens. As good stewards of God's resources, we have to grow from the point of attempting to handle everything on our own and get to the point of taking personal responsibility for our own plight and seeking out the appropriate resources and support to accomplish our goals. We must stop lying to ourselves or minimizing our financial situation and accept the fact that the choices and decisions we've made up to this point have resulted in the consequences we're currently facing. We must realize and embrace the things we do well and demonstrate humility by asking for help in the areas where we do not excel.

> $$$ The key to conquering financial strongholds is to admit that there's a problem, accept that you don't have all the answers, and change your mind about remaining a victim.

## Sense of Entitlement

There's an epidemic that is rampant and rapidly shaping the way individuals, students, employees and Christian believers think. It's the sense of entitlement. There seems to be an inexplicable, unsubstantiated expectation that somebody somewhere owes us something. And it's not true.

Selfish entitlement has a long and dark history that we can trace back to the Old Testament. In the parable of the prodigal son found in Luke 15:11-32, we are introduced to a young man who is characterized by greed, impatience, and a sense of entitlement that he somehow is deserving of something he hasn't worked for or earned – his father's inheritance. The prodigal son is a good example of a lost sheep in need of a Financial Shepherd to help him understand and appreciate the value of money and resources. Like so many of us, he suffered from dissatisfaction and a spirit of discontentment. When people feel dissatisfied with their lot in life, we can trace it to misplacement of value regarding what's really important in life. Matthew 6:21 (ESV) states, "For where your treasure is, there your heart will be also." Where is your treasure? What do you value? Do you suffer from a spirit of discontentment and feel entitled to things you haven't earned? Notice that when the Bible makes references to matters of the heart, it includes one's thoughts, behaviors, and emotions. So in essence, changing the way we think will ultimately result in a change of heart.

Many people feel they are owed something because of a historical legacy or oppression that has been inflicted upon specific groups of people. Others think they are owed something because of certain things they have gone through, experienced, or endured. I think back to growing up in my neighborhood and seeing people who were stuck in financially dire situations complaining about what the government was or was not doing to them and for them. Even in the workplace, there are those who feel that because they've been loyal to a company for 20 or 30 years, that it automatically entitles them to something that was never promised. Even young people who haven't yet had to earn a living or pay their dues in life feel that they should automatically reap the benefits of their parents' hard work - without putting forth any effort themselves. Today's airwaves are literally filled with Reality TV episodes featuring pseudo-celebrities that feel entitled to fame and fortune although they possess no easily discernable skills or talent and exhibit nothing more than the ability to sensationalize the mundane. The truth is that nobody owes you anything.

Americans live in a world defined by a sense of entitlement. After World War II, while the rest of the world recovered, the United States forged ahead and exploded into an era of manufacturing and economic growth. As a result, the new economic stability laid the groundwork for

American staples such as Social Security and Medicare. People began to rely on these funds and then built their lives and retirements around the idea that they would always exist. For decades, government subsidies like Social Security, Medicare, and pensions have been taken for granted as automatic lifelines that would always be in place as financial safety nets. But that is no longer the case. There are no more guarantees, and the reality check of self-reliance is underscoring the harsh reality that no one is entitled to anything anymore.

There was a time when paying bills on time was not an option. Individuals and families understood that if you couldn't afford to pay for it in cash, then you just couldn't afford it yet. And instead of overextending themselves with credit and digging a deeper hole of debt, they just saved money and waited until they could afford it. Such occurrences are uncommon these days. Now we are all suffering as a result with record-high consumer credit losses, unprecedented national debt, unmanageable debt-to-income ratios, and underwater mortgages for homes inhabited by debt-ridden families surviving on credit to compete with people they don't know by buying things they don't really want or need. Indeed, the sense of entitlement has buried an entire generation under a load of debt that will take decades to uncover and reverse.

Ironically, modern Americans have the absolute highest standard of living in the history of mankind, and yet there still seems to be a sense of dissatisfaction and a desire for more, more, more. Top U.S. earners make more money in a month than individuals in low-wealth nations make all year, and yet it still isn't enough. Corporations and industries have shown such significant growth, they've literally been billed as "too big to fail," yet they still send jobs overseas and lay off workers for a bigger bottom line and profit margin. People in general have more material goods than ever, yet repeatedly report the highest levels of clinically diagnosed depression. The sense of entitlement that drives people to acquire more and more still has yet to prove that money makes you happy. It doesn't.

## Change Your Mind, Change Your Life

So, what is your personal motivation for financial freedom? If you think that more money will make you happy, then you are sadly mistaken. If you think that money is the answer to your marriage, family, or relationship issues, then you are wrong. Changing how you think about money is a crucial step in achieving financial freedom. Knowing that God is your first priority is the key to success as stated in Matthew 6:33 (KJV), "But seek ye first the kingdom of God and his righteousness, and all these things shall be added unto you."

Do you know who you are? Body. Soul. Spirit. You are a unique individual made of the past, living in the present, and preparing for the future. You are more than your bank account. You are more than your title. You are more than your net worth. You are more than what other people think or say about you. You are fearfully and wonderfully made in the image of God. You are who He says you are.

Many people are dominated and consumed with a former version of themselves. If you talk to them about anything, their entire point of reference is from some great accomplishment or achievement in the past, but they have never grown beyond that point which ultimately hinders them from achieving more and advancing to the level of Financial Shepherding and mentoring others. These individuals are so focused on what and who they used to be, that they are missing out on who they are now, and who they are destined to be in the future.

I have met people in their 40s and 50s and held conversations with them that centered solely on things that happened 20 or 25 years ago. They reminisce about their first corporate job, or that big promotion decades ago, or making some big first-time purchase like a car or home. As a result of not being able to break through their financial ceiling, they've maintained an emotional attachment to the past that prevents them from achieving the necessary relevant goals for the present, or even correctly positioning themselves for the future. In addition, when I meet some of the individuals in their inner circle - or who are part of their personal financial resource management team, those individuals think just like them and are also trapped under a collapsing financial ceiling from which they cannot escape.

People who constantly live in the past tend to stay there and are often resistant to change or the entrance of new knowledge, information, or challenges because it means they have to grow and accept that things will be different. It also means they sometimes have to let go of how things used to be and adapt to the things that are. That transition can often be frightening or unnerving, so many people ignore or attempt to avoid change all together. In order to let go of the past and move forward, we must rely on our faith in God to propel us toward the destiny He has prepared.

The present-minded folks tend to focus on learning as much as possible about their current situation, exploring their options, and pursuing a plan of action that propels them toward their goals. People focused on the present tend to be proactive at taking an honest assessment of where they are; changing what can be changed and asking for help when they need it. To some extent, we are all present-based thinkers because we are all striving to excel and make the best of our situation today.

The optimal place in life is to have a good perspective on the past, a good grasp on the present, and to be future-focused; that is, paying attention to changing trends and taking advantage of opportunities on the financial horizon. Most entrepreneurs tend to be future-based thinkers. They function as if there is always an opportunity they can seize to make things better and the future brighter. Even though many entrepreneurs are financially independent, they continue to work hard or start new businesses because they love the challenge and thrill of seeing new ventures successfully materialize. They are continually focused on the possibility of what can be. Future-focused people understand that change is inevitable, so it is necessary to adapt your thinking and plan for the known and the unknown. Future-focused people understand that now is as good a time as any to position themselves for success.

## Chapter 8 – Plan Your Financial Future

Now, it is time to put in the work. Chapters 10 and 11 will prepare you for the planning process and then map out the strategies and technical information you need to know to make good financial decisions. Get ready to learn a lot. Get ready to apply what you've learned. Get ready to move further down the path toward financial freedom and continue the process that has already started.

The financial information you gain from reading this book will start you on the journey to developing "a new you." There is no better time than the present to start on this financial safari that is going to change the rest of your life. By following God's plan, you are going to learn life lessons that will finally break the bonds of financial limitations on your life. If you feel like you aren't happy where you are or with the past decisions that you've made, then this is the plan for you. Once you master these divine principles, you will have more happiness, more peace, more confidence, and more money. Nothing is more rewarding than unleashing your God-given abilities and potential to live a purposeful life. Understand that it does not matter what the problem is, all things are possible when God is involved.

[Sy] *Prepare to Work Your Plan*
**1. Assessing Your Money Motivation**
This is where we reassess your overall perspective as it relates to money. In the previous chapters we challenged you to change the way you think about money. This includes your personal obligations and your commitment to effectively managing what God has allowed you to oversee. We have stated that the earth—and everything in it—belongs to the Heavenly

Father and that Jesus Christ is the Chief Financial Shepherd. Do you truly understand that everything belongs to God? How does this affect your future financial decisions? What is your perspective on tithing and giving? Do you understand the role and purpose of a Financial Shepherd? Are you committed to eventually becoming a Financial Shepherd and sharing the knowledge and wisdom that you've gained? Do you understand your personal role in becoming a Financial Shepherd and helping develop others? What are some potential road blocks that may prevent you from becoming a Financial Shepherd? Who makes up your team of wise counselors? What other questions or concerns do you have about Financial Shepherding? In order to provide the most effective comprehensive financial plan, your money motivation must match that of the Financial Shepherd. Akin to shepherds of real sheep, the Financial Shepherd's "rod or staff" is his or her comprehensive financial plan.

Debt and indebtedness are contentious issues that require the light of spiritual truth. Although debt is a reality, it is not reflective of God's character. He owns everything, so essentially all are indebted to Him. But when we think of the debt that we acquire as consumers, we must look at how we got into our individual situations. As we discussed in a previous chapter, most debt comes as a result of poor spending habits, greed, and emotional spending. It can also be the result of "generational curses." This is when debt is inherited or the behaviors and thought patterns that lead to debt are encouraged by those that were influential in our upbringing. When one is drowning in debt, it is possible to be consumed with your financial affairs in such a way that paying your tithes becomes more and more difficult. The reality is that you may not have sufficient funds, but this should not discourage you from being obedient to God.

If you cannot pay the full tithe, while you are working your plan to get out of debt, we encourage you to give as much as you can. In addition, you can also offer volunteer service to your church or ministry and assist the people who make up the church congregation in different areas of need until you are able to recover financially. This is only a temporary solution, and not a substitute for tithing. As believers, we are to give our full tithe, talent, and treasure to support the work of God's kingdom. The truth of the matter is, as believers, we cannot afford not to tithe.

**2. Financial Coaching**

Since our overall aim is to help you increase your level of self awareness and to assist you with changing the way you think about your finances, a *financial assessment/ money personality profile* is a good first step. We typically use this tool to help develop your comprehensive financial plan and to make recommendations that may be beneficial for you and your family along the way. Although, financial coaching is not necessary for every client, it is recommended for those that are fighting the battle for financial freedom.

Previously we talked about changing the way you think, exploring irrational behaviors, and the genetic and environmental factors that affect the decisions you make. The theoretical perspective that we've observed to be most effective when exploring thoughts and behaviors is Cognitive Behavioral Therapy (CBT) and Reality Therapy. The type of coaching or counseling needed depends upon your current situation. Individual coaching is when the coach and the client establish a therapeutic rapport in a one-on-one therapy setting. The sessions are confidential and are personalized according to the needs of the client. Marriage and family counseling is designed for the respective client base and should be facilitated in an objective manner. Individual counseling is often recommended for married couples and the individual members of families as well, to address issues that may need further personal exploration. Various personality inventories (if applicable), also will help the counselor assist you in the therapy sessions. It is important to remember that we all have certain limitations and areas that we are much stronger in than others. Financial coaching and family counseling are avenues to help you draw upon those strengths and use them to overcome the obstacles that can stand in the way of your success. One of the greatest strengths of the Financial Shepherd as well as those that are on the path to becoming a Financial Shepherd is recognizing that we need others to be successful. As you prepare to engage in counseling/coaching, here are some common questions to consider.

How do I teach my children about money? Teaching children how to become Financial Shepherds starts before they know anything about money. It starts with the toys and the belongings that parents provide for them. As parents, we should teach our children to take care of the things that belong to others even better than their own things. Notice this change from the mindset of our society. Essentially everything belongs to God, so we should tell them "everything belongs to God "i.e., the house, cars, money, everything! Since this is the case, we are to take care of God's possessions better than our own. Children are more impressionable, so this will sink in sooner than you realize.

In addition, it's important to use age-appropriate language with children and help them understand the value of work. Allowances are fine, but they should be attached to accomplishment, so that children start to comprehend the relationship between work and reward. Make sure your child has a piggy bank and a bank account so that they learn the importance of saving. Finally, teach your children how to give, so they do not become selfish and self-centered and grow up perpetuating that practice. The most important way to teach this principle to children is for parents to live it daily. When you change the way you act, live, and think about finances, those that depend on you and follow your lead will also have a changed mindset.

My spouse and I have different spending habits, how do we compromise and start communicating about money? First, married couples should be aware that this is a common theme in marriages. When individuals marry after being independent for a number of years, their personal goals need to be readjusted from focusing on "me" to "we." In my practice as a therapist, conflict involving money is the problem presented most often by married couples. Money is important in marriage but it should never be what a marriage is based upon. In fact, if the marriage is based upon anything other than Christ, the conflict will manifest itself through that substitute.

Marriages based on anything other than Christ are conditional marriages, and unfortunately, they are motivated by the nature of the source. For example, if a couple marries because of their physical attraction to one another, what happens when the attraction fades? Or if the marriage is based upon emotions, what happens when the emotions change? This should be addressed during the premarital counseling process, but at this point, I would recommend supportive counseling to address the issues of concern. Oftentimes the cause of the problem may present as "different spending habits," but in actuality the root problem is something more in-depth, such as a power or control issue.

I would also advise the couple to review our Four C's of Financial Success: Consciousness, Communication, Commitment, and Clarity. Notice that the word "compromise" did not make the list. Couples must agree on like goals, but this is not a matter of compromising. When you are joined together in Holy matrimony, you work together as one to accomplish the same goals.

## The Four C's of Financial Success

Consciousness, communication, commitment, and clarity are four keys to financial success. Keep in mind that every choice you make has an economic consequence. When you master these four financial concepts, every financial decision you make will be better. It is amazing how each "C" appears to interlock with the others and to open the door for the next one. We can rank them from first to last, but neither "C" appears to stand as strong without the others.

**Consciousness** - Merriam-Webster dictionary defines consciousness as "the quality or state of being aware especially of something within oneself." Just as goals are the most important part of planning, self awareness is the emotional catalyst for being successful. When you know who you are, you then have a base to build upon. More importantly when you know *whose* you are in Christ, you know that your foundation is firmly planted and immovable.

In addition to being self-aware, there must also be an acceptance of the need to change and do things differently than in the past. Often something bad happens to make us aware that things are going wrong, which then provides the motivation we need for change. For instance, we had a friend growing up who bought whatever he wanted whenever he wanted and didn't save anything. As we grew older he bought more and more stuff and piled up more and more debt. Then one day his car was repossessed because he fell behind on the payments. He was so embarrassed. But that's when he realized that he was handling his finances the wrong way, and he vowed never to spend so recklessly again. He vowed to make a change once he became acutely aware and conscious of the problem.

**Communication** - Effective communication is a dual pathway that allows us to collect and disperse information during the process of expressing and exchanging our ideas, thoughts, and feelings. However, if we're unwilling or unable to adequately express our concerns, it creates difficulty for everyone involved. The truth is that it is almost impossible to fix any problem that you are unwilling to talk about. And at the core of most challenges—especially within the area of finances—is poor or non-existent communication. Contrary to popular belief, ignoring financial problems does not make them go away.

The first step to more effective communication is to develop some "rules of order." For example, a crucial rule in financial communication is total honesty about debt, income, bills, beliefs, values, and spiritual understanding of the role of finances. Pretending to believe or support something just to avoid an argument will only create a bigger argument down the road. Another communication tool is to see the other person's perspective by considering what it's like in their shoes. If one spouse grew up poor with nothing extra to save for a rainy day, it may explain why they don't place a high value on savings and investments. Their perspective needs to broaden to understand why these things are important. If the other spouse inherited wealth that they did not have to work for, they may not appreciate budgeting because they've never had to do it. But that individual needs to understand the value of budgeting and accountability in case he or she encounters difficult times in their finances in the future. Once you understand why someone does the things they do, you can help them consider new ways of thinking and making decisions - if you are willing to communicate honestly about them.

**Commitment** - Traditionally, commitment tends to be the most difficult of the Four C's of Financial Success. It is much easier to maintain a noncommittal stance, because it leaves you free from any obligations. When we explore the minds of those that avoid commitment, we learn that they fear the vulnerabilities that may come as a result of some type of attachment (i.e., relationships). In order to overcome this fear, you must look to the first two C's- consciousness and communication. Without any awareness of this tendency, a client is unable to communicate the need to change it. Once these first two C's have been established, only then can we place emphasis on the benefits of commitment. When we look at commitment in the financial realm, it's a matter of recognizing that there may be some challenging times along the way. If your goal happens to be saving to buy a new home, then there is a level of commitment that you must make in order to see this goal come to fruition. Depending upon your financial profile, you may have to make some changes to the spending habits that you have grown accustomed to. But the end result is always in direct correlation with the level of commitment. No one said that this process was going to be easy. We didn't get in debt overnight, so we will not get out overnight. People who are considered overnight sensations and get their millions "quickly" normally don't. They spend their lives preparing for the opportunity that God will provide. The key is to stay committed to your goal.

**Clarity** - 'Where there is no vision, the people perish' (Proverbs 29:18a). When it comes to financial planning, it is imperative to have a specific goal and a clear plan on how to get where you want to go. Goals and plans must be clear or you simply will not achieve them. You have to be able to see yourself out of debt and financially free. Quite simply, to have clarity is to know where we stand and where we want to be. Success always comes as the result of a clear vision.

Now that you have properly assessed your money motivation and have an understanding of the Four C's of Financial Success, it's time to list your primary goals. A good way to determine if you're on the right track is to use the S.M.A.R.T. goal guidelines. For example, a **S**pecific, **M**easureable, **A**ttainable, **R**ealistic, **T**imely financial goal can be stated as follows: "Save at least $200 per month for 12 months to build up my emergency savings account at *ABC Bank*."

Another example might be: "Research and interview at least three financial planners and open a new investment account by June."

**List your top five S.M.A.R.T. financial goals:**

| |
|---|
| 1. |
| 2. |
| 3. |
| 4. |
| 5. |

### On Your Mark, Get Set, Go!

How many times have we heard someone say, "If you fail to plan, then you plan to fail?" Well, in actuality, there is a lot of truth in that statement because not having a financial plan is the equivalent of throwing darts in the dark or basically leaving your financial future up to chance.

My experiences as an athlete and as a college basketball coach have enabled me to learn and develop skills that I have been able to use on the court and in real life situations. It was during my coaching years that I realized how the lack of a plan or being ill-prepared can be detrimental to your future. Knowing what play to call when you are down by two points with eight seconds to go in a double overtime game does not matter if you have not practiced (planned) a play to run for that very situation.

Perhaps the most important part of any type of plan is the goal-setting process. Our goals provide a mark to aim towards, or better yet, a direction to advance. They also bring about the structure that is necessary to plan successfully. When I was a college basketball player, every year I knew that our coach would call a team meeting prior to the season to make sure we were all mentally on the same page. As a team of players and coaches, we would write out our goals and the objectives that it took to reach each one. Our coach would then copy the goals and post them on our lockers so that we could see them and be reminded daily of what we were planning to do. It's amazing how the basic tenets of goal-setting can be used in sports, academics, and with your finances. What's even more amazing is how the Bible similarly used an example of an athlete in scripture to help me apply these same principles to my own life.

First, you have to have a goal to work toward. Having no goal is like walking in the dark with a blindfold on. It's not possible to see in the dark even when your eyes are not covered, but when you don't have any directions or plans to get out of the dark, then you choose to cover your own eyes (blindfolded) and you choose to continue to wander aimlessly. We have to follow the example the Apostle Paul set for us in 1 Corinthians 9:26, "Therefore I run in such a way, as not without aim; I box in such a way, as not beating the air." Second, your goal(s) must embody the principle of sowing and reaping. Simply put, you will get out of something what you put into it.

I like the way the Message version of 1 Corinthians 9:26-27 communicates this principle: "I don't know about you, but I'm running hard for the finish line. I'm giving it everything I've got. No sloppy living for me! I'm staying alert and in top condition. I'm not going to get caught napping, telling everyone else all about it and then missing out myself."

And last, your goal(s) should always put you in a position to be successful. 1 Corinthians 9:24b tells us to "Run in such a way that you may win." What is the purpose of setting a goal if you do not have plans to attain it in the first place? Why set a goal if you don't expect to be successful?"

> $$$ A crucial rule in financial communication is total honesty about debt, income, bills, beliefs, values, and spiritual understanding of the role of finances

[Glen]   Without question, we know the key first step in financial planning is goal-setting. By setting new goals, one acquires a new sense of purpose. We routinely encourage our clients to consider and develop a plan for their life dreams - and most importantly - to dream big. As believers, when we put our dreams in God's hands, we are able to observe and experience the miraculous.

One of the other resulting consequences of setting goals is that we are forced to establish new relationships and develop new financial habits. New relationships provide us with greater opportunities and better results. I remember the first time I wanted to get in shape. I had never exercised a day in my life, but once I started, it felt great and I lost 10 pounds. I loved my lighter self, so I continued to do the same thing over and over until I hit a plateau. So then I decided that I needed to increase my goal and lose 10 more pounds. I didn't know how I would do it, but I knew I wanted to do it because I was still vastly overweight. So I prayed about it, and literally the next week, a friend of mine who I considered to look like the Incredible Hulk told me he was moving to my side of town and asked me if there was a good gym nearby. I told him my gym was great, and I asked if I could train with him sometime. He agreed and three months later I lost an additional 25 pounds. I was in the best shape of my life. My friend gave me the support I needed to reach my new goals. The development of that new relationship forced me to establish a new routine and adopt new, healthy habits that helped achieve my fitness and weight loss goals. The same principles that applied to health and wellness also apply to financial fitness.

New personal habits allow us to obtain higher levels of achievement. By changing old habits, you tend to leave the old complexities of life behind. In order to work out with my friend, I had to wake up at 4:30 in the morning. I normally slept until 6:30 everyday, so this was quite an adjustment. After I decided to do that, I found myself benefiting in many other ways. First, I lost weight and I felt more confident. Second, I became more disciplined in other ways, like how I ate. It even enhanced my work ethic. I was now the first person at work every day and I really got a lot done before my employees arrived at the office in the morning. Previously, I had been working on weekends just to keep up, but now I was able to have my weekends to myself and not have to think about work. I didn't make time to stop at the doughnut store before work any longer, instead I made smoothies and other healthy snacks at home. As a result, I saved money and calories. This extra time, energy, and confidence allowed me to be in places and meet people that I probably would not have encountered if I hadn't set specific goals and then created a detailed plan to follow them based on renewed relationships and habits.

When setting goals, we must be careful to avoid measuring our success against the attainments of others. In our respective practices, we counsel and encourage our clients to 'Measure From Behind'. This means to look back and see just how far you've come, and how far God has brought you, based upon your own accomplishments. Our recommended strategy is to measure your own progress by your own progress and growth - not by anyone else.

Many of us watch television and desire to imitate and emulate what we see. The question becomes, 'if Donald Trump has a Rolls Royce then why can't I have one too?' Well, it may be the case that you didn't grow up with a father like Donald Trump's who was already a wealthy man and who also passed along his wealth, access, contacts, network, and financial knowledge to his son. So, if you don't have those circumstances, that can't be your plan. Success similar to Mr. Trump's can be your goal, but you will need to develop your own plan or roadmap to get you there. So, the bottom line is that it's not that you can't have similar success; it's just that your plan has to work for you.

Although we plan for the future, we do occasionally have to look back to truly measure our progress. We all have an ideal of where we would like to see ourselves, and it may seem to be a long way away. But don't be discouraged, because we measure progress from behind by creating forward motion that is headed toward a specific goal. In the process, we are reminded of where God has brought us from, and thankful to Him for His goodness and blessings each step of the way. We must always remember to celebrate the "small things" along the way.

Growing up in church, I used to always hear pastors preach about having an "attitude of gratitude." I never knew how important that phrase was until I witnessed one of my clients who seemingly had it all suffer in miserable isolation because he always wanted more and was never truly grateful for what he already had.

Steven* always wanted to start his own internet and technology firm and become a wealthy, successful CEO like many of the other famous tech geniuses whose names frequent business headlines. Steven did all the right things, met all the right people, and successfully climbed up the corporate ladder towards success. We started working together when he was in his 20s, and by the time he turned 35, he was a millionaire. He had traveled all over the world and always had a story about the celebrities and dignitaries he had met and spent time with. He won awards for leadership and success, and was constantly recognized by his colleagues and peers in his field. Yet, that was never enough. Despite all the accolades and financial success, Steven is one of the unhappiest people I know. Instead of "measuring from behind" and seeing how far he has come, he still compares himself to individuals who are richer and more famous, causing him to focus on what he doesn't have instead of what he does. The tragedy is that Steven may spend his entire life trying to follow someone else's plan that will never work for him - because he isn't them.

If you are willing to change your mind, you can change your destiny and reap the benefits of God's perfect plan for *your* life. But all of us must be willing to accept that we don't know everything – and that sometimes we may need to ask for help. Finding a good Financial Shepherd is a step in the right direction when it comes to getting on track. As a matter of fact, that person should then inspire you to become a Financial Shepherd to lead and mentor others. We also need to embrace an attitude of gratitude and learn to appreciate what we have and enjoy the journey while we grow into our destiny of success. As one of my favorite quotations states, "You cannot walk into your future backwards." Look ahead and envision the wonderful life God has planned for you when you seek Him first.

*"If you don't know where you are going, any road will get you there."*
*~Lewis Carroll*

## Chapter 9 – Your Financial Plan is Personal

**Cash Management and Investment Strategies**

[Glen] Get out your highlighter and prepare to initiate your new financial plan. There are not a lot of stories or anecdotes in this chapter. Instead, there is a lot of technical information to inform and equip you to meet your short-term and long-term financial goals.

If you have questions about any of the terms listed, look for definitions and in-depth explanations in Chapter 14, *Blessed to Be a Blessing*, where we include the Top 50 Financial Terms you should know.

**$ $ Financial Planning Begins Here $ $**

*Cash Management Strategies-* More than just balancing your checkbook, cash management includes creating and following a **budget**, **using credit wisely**, and **keeping your income tax burden at the lowest level possible**. Even if you think you do not yet make enough money to concern yourself with tax rates and tax management, you must begin to think and act like where you want to be. The goal is to help you control your spending and manage your money as other successful and affluent Financial Shepherds.

*Budgeting-* The main purpose for the budget is to plan how someone's money will be spent. Since most of us have limited resources, budgeting provides a way for us to monitor and manage personal cash flow, and to meet both current and future needs. Everyone needs a budget, regardless of how much or how little money they have, because everyone needs to have a solid understanding of their individual financial position. Following the example of the wealthy, it is important to know that most affluent people have an excellent understanding of their personal budget and a keen awareness of how money comes in and where money goes out.

In creating a budget, start with research and fact-finding to get a good assessment of what is your true financial situation. Use the information you discover to record all details about past cash flow, both income and spending. Paycheck stubs, check registers, tax returns, and receipts are all great sources of information. For those individuals who are advanced in budgeting, the preference is to use reward-based credit cards that provide annual statements. For those new to this process, we are not referring to store-based credit cards or debit cards. Reward cards offer a return-on-investment for purchases made or goods and services that are used, hence adding to your cash management and savings plan. Using a good reward card wisely can save you hundreds or thousands of dollars per year in addition to providing excellent records for tracking and categorizing your expenditures. If you already have a household budget in place, make sure it is updated with all current bills, loans, and other financial obligations. If you are just beginning to budget, begin with the steps below.

Step 1: Set goals in three categories. Short, Intermediate, and Long-Term. Short- term financial goals include saving toward emergency reserves, vacations, or anything planned within 24 months or less. Intermediate goals are between 2-10 years. The goals may include saving for a new car, saving for a new home, or planning for a child's college education if the child is older than 8 years old. Ironically, even though intermediate goals tend to have the highest price tag, this category of financial planning is the one people are least likely to do. As a result, deficits in these areas tend to spill over into short- and long-term goals and negatively impact financial planning for immediate and future endeavors. Finally, long-term planning encompasses retirement, estate planning, and college education funds for children under the age of 8. Long-term planning entails any financial aspirations beyond 10 years from now.

Step 2: Maintain your records. This can be difficult, but it is very necessary in order to get a good grasp of what amount of money comes in and goes out each month. We recommend using the credit card option because it is helpful in keeping and maintaining a system of good record-keeping. In the hustle and bustle of appointments and deadlines, we often forget the quick lunch meeting receipt or coffee shop expense that remain unaccounted for in our budget. Then, at the end of the month, we're left wondering what happened to our money. Paying for items using credit and debit cards makes record-keeping and financial accountability very easy. Part of being obedient to God's plan and becoming a Financial Shepherd is being <u>transparent</u> with your budget. So if you are going over this with your financial planner or spouse, <u>make sure you discuss the entire budget</u>.

Step 3: Finally, there must be a periodic review of the past, present, and future to monitor your financial progress. Your budget must be monitored daily in the beginning, and as you grow, budget reviews can become less frequent and occur weekly, and then monthly. Everyone needs to monitor their spending no less than on a monthly basis. This practice will help identify what is going well and what you need to change before it's too late.

*Spending Habits*: Recent tough economic times have taught us that we are not entitled to everything we want just because we want it – and feel like we deserve it. Therefore, we have to stop spending like we have a God-given right to get anything and everything we want in life. I meet with people all the time who say "I deserve this" or "I deserve that." But in order to achieve financial freedom, you must stop thinking about what you think you deserve and start thinking about what you can afford. I once met a woman who grew up very poor. She worked hard and was the first in her family to graduate from college. She even received a master's degree. She was single and earned approximately $95,000 a year, plus a benefits package [$1 for $1 match in 401(k)] for every dollar up to $15,000 per year, which is almost unheard of. However, she consistently shopped for luxury cars, clothes, and only ate at the best restaurants with her friends. Over time, she became complacent and began to feel as though she was entitled to the "good life" she had acquired. She stopped contributing to her retirement plan and eventually fell into huge credit card debt. When asked about her situation, her reply was, "I deserve it because of where I came from and all my hard work." That simply was not true. As a result of her attitude about money and her refusal to *change* her actions and spending habits, she ended up making a lot of poor decisions with her money that didn't make *sense*. Eventually, she paid a very high price for her failure to heed wise counsel and get her priorities in line with God's priorities for her life. When it comes to finances and spiritual accountability, we need to be clear that God's plan and His purpose for our lives do not include foolish excess on one extreme or constantly being broke and in debt at the other extreme. As a matter of fact, these are the types of situations that can keep you from reaching His destiny for you. But ultimately, we are given choices to make that have very real consequences to face. Unfortunately for this individual, she chose the path of self-entitlement, and it led to financial devastation for her.

If you find that you consistently have more month than money, you are going to have to eliminate the "wants and desires" in your budget and focus spending on "needs" instead. This means that you may have to eliminate going out to lunch during the work week, wash your own hair, or mow your own lawn. If that's not enough, you may have to turn off the home phone if you have a cell phone, reduce and monitor other utilities, and go without excessive luxuries that are not really necessities. For example, do you really need the HDTV cable package with all the extra movie channels? Consider letting it go and getting one step closer to your dream of financial freedom. Simple adjustments like raising the deductible on your health and automobile insurance plans can assist in reducing unnecessary expenses. You potentially could save 10 to 20 percent (or more) on your insurance premiums just by raising your deductible levels from $250 to $1,000.

**Debt Reduction/Emergency Savings Fund**

Although many financial "experts" may tell you to focus on paying off debt first, this is the wrong approach. Certainly, the goal is to pay off debts (especially bad debt), but at the same time, we must always save for emergencies and unforeseen situations that require a quick cash resolution e.g., automobile repairs, medical co-payments for unexpected injuries, or charitable contributions to local organizations to help support the community. I have witnessed countless clients, friends, and family members pay off all their credit cards – building little to no savings – and then ending up right back in debt again due to some household emergency.

By saving money and reducing debt simultaneously, the end result produces financial freedom, improved credit, and a comfortable cushion. Most people who follow this plan get out of debt and stay out of debt for good.

> **$$$ What to do:** *Calculate your total living expenses for an entire month (mortgage, rent, groceries, utilities, transportation, insurance, medical, etc.) then set a goal to save enough money to cover six months worth of expenses – with the ultimate goal of saving enough to cover at least 12 months of expenses.

*Note: If you have a high-interest-rate credit card, and no 6- to 12-month emergency reserve fund, then start paying the minimum amount due on the credit card every month (on time or early) and start saving for your emergency reserve fund. Remember, emergencies do happen, and you need to be prepared.

It is important to understand debt and types of debt in order to take control over it. It is important to realize that there is good debt and bad debt.

> $$$ Borrowing money for the purpose of FINANCIAL LEVERAGING is the only acceptable reason you should ever borrow money at all!

**Good debt** occurs as a result of investing in an asset that should appreciate (go up in value) over a period of time. Most of us understand that our current federal tax code favors wealthy individuals. Therefore we need to take advantage of the opportunities and follow suit. Good debt can be deductible (check with your tax advisor first) on your taxes. Examples of this would be mortgages to buy real estate, margin accounts to buy more stock, and some student loans to pay for higher education. College costs are almost always a good investment for long-term growth since statistics prove that college graduates have a consistently higher earning potential than those with a high school degree only.

**Bad debt** encompasses virtually every other situation with the exceptions of financial leveraging and asset investments. Beware of emotional purchases and desperation loans to "tide you over." We've all heard about predatory lending agencies that frequently exploit those who are in dire financial straits. Loans for income tax refunds are the worst! There is no reason you should ever pay as much as $500 to get your check the same day, versus getting a direct deposit a week later. If I'm talking to you, please don't do this again. Work on spending less, saving more, reducing debt and opening a bank account with an established, FDIC-insured (Federal Deposit Insurance Corporation) financial institution.

Beware of furniture loans, clothing store debt, auto loans (hate those too), check cashing/payday loans, 401(k) or any retirement plan loan (horrible, because you're being taxed twice). All of these are financial traps to avoid. Understandably, if you're digging out of a financial ditch, you may already be ensnared by some of these money-making schemes. However, as your plan progresses, the objective is to weed them out of your overall financial strategy. Take some time to review this sample debt-reduction strategy and then use it to develop your own plan along with your financial planner.

A good place to start with debt-reduction and cash management is to create additional income that isn't already accounted for in your budget. With those extra funds, you can assign them to specific bills or high-interest credit cards or debt and increase your debt reduction rate. Here are some ways to "create" extra income:

*a. Change your W-4 tax withholdings status.* There are many people who wait to get a huge tax refund in January; however, this is not good money management. Not only are you giving Uncle Sam an interest-free loan on your hard-earned money, but you are also missing out on an opportunity to invest those funds yourself and reap the benefits of your own hard work. For example, instead of receiving a refund for $4,800, decrease your total withholdings, save that $400 per month, and invest it in a high-interest financial account and profit hundreds of dollars over time – instead of just taking an interest-free lump sum amount. That money can be used for the dream vacation you've been wishing for or some other nice luxury. Of course, if you are in debt, you should use that $400 per month to pay it down, thus saving in additional interest costs and fees.

*b. Reduce the monthly total of your bills.* You can accomplish this goal by becoming more energy-efficient and reducing usage of utilities. Turn off lights in empty rooms and unplug electronics that are not in use. If possible, make use of public transportation to reduce transportation costs and vehicle maintenance costs caused by excessive wear and tear on your car. Get rid of unnecessary expenses like cable television or satellite networks altogether until you've managed to get out of debt and save enough to cover extra "wants" and luxury expenses. Even if you're not behind on your bills, it is still possible to get a reduction in interest rates on many store credit cards by simply making a call to the Customer Service department and asking for a lower rate. The current economic environment has elevated the art of bargaining and negotiating, so it definitely will not hurt to ask. Even large companies are willing to reduce an interest rate now if it means keeping a good, timely-paying customer. When you're trying to pay down debt, every dollar and cent matter.

*c. Consider moonlighting to earn extra income.* Don't overlook the possibility of temporarily taking on a second job, part-time job, or generating extra income from a home-based business. Over the years we've worked with clients who simply spent more than they made and needed to create a new revenue source to undo the damage done. One of the biggest obstacles for many people in considering a second job is the pride factor. However, it is much more respectable to get a second job for a short time and live debt free as opposed to living paycheck to paycheck, putting on a front, and pretending everything is fine just to look good to other people. It's just not worth it.

 *d. Check your credit card and bank statements monthly.* It is also important to check your credit report and credit score a couple of times a year to make sure there aren't any mistakes that may work against you. If you do find an incorrect charge on your credit card, report it to the company immediately and document any correspondence or conversations until the situation has been satisfactorily resolved by crediting the charge and any interest accrued back to you. A recent report showed that the majority of people have at least one error on their credit report that indicates a negative reporting which can potentially lower their credit score or prevent them from securing additional credit in the future. Make reviewing your credit and bank statements a routine part of your financial plan.

 *e. Refinance your debt.* If you cannot call and get a lower interest rate, you may need to refinance your debt. If you have a high-interest-rate credit card, then you should look for offers from another card to lower that rate. Word to the wise, be careful because many credit cards have low interest rates for a short period of time, and then they revert back to rates where you were before or maybe even higher than before. In addition, make sure you watch the balance transfer fees that companies charge. Refinancing depreciable assets (such as a car) and paying unnecessary interest payments need to be avoided at all costs. Financial moves such as those decrease your overall net worth because you almost always become upside-down in value. If you are considering refinancing your home, make sure that you recoup the costs of the refinance before you move. For instance, there is no reason to refinance and pay 3 to 4 percent in closing costs if you plan to move within a year. Throughout your decision-making process, make sure the monthly savings outweigh the costs. Also, take your savings and apply it toward your debt after you have built up your emergency savings.

 *f. Consolidate loans.* Sometimes it is a good idea to consolidate your loans - especially student loans and many credit cards. It especially makes sense when you can lower your interest rates. Also, refinancing should help with cash flow, because your payment on this one loan should be less than if you were paying all of them individually. If you have equity in your home, a Home Equity Line of Credit (HELOC) makes sense as a source of credit for loan consolidation. Since you are borrowing money from an asset the bank can securitize (something they can confiscate or take away if you don't pay), the bank takes less risk. Because of the reduced risk, the interest rate most likely will be in your favor. For example, paying off a credit card that has a 20 percent interest rate with a refinanced HELOC at 5 percent makes a lot more sense because you will have lower payments and also save on interest. Also, if refinancing is for your primary residence, the interest should be tax-deductible (check with your tax advisor to find out what's approved in your state of residence). Keep in mind that this is only for extreme circumstances because of the risk involved. You must take into consideration what would happen if you lost your job or your primary source of income. With the debt being attached to your home, the inability to fulfill your payment obligations may cause you to lose your home (secured debt) versus if it was just a credit card (unsecured debt). Like everything, there are pros and cons associated with every strategy or tactic for reducing debt, so carefully weigh all your options and discuss all scenarios with your financial planner to find the best strategy for you.

 g. *Reposition your assets.* Sometimes we have to use cash or sell things in order to get rid of excess debt. Because gold prices are at an all-time high, I have seen many people receive thousands of dollars selling unwanted gold to pay off bills and pay down debt. In fact, I personally sold some gold jewelry I've owned since high school and college (that I would never wear again) and received almost the same amount I paid for it years ago. Don't forget that you can sell that extra car, rental property, or even securities to pay off debt.

 *(Again, there may be tax implications for some transactions, so make sure you speak with your tax advisor first.)*

Now that you've identified ways to create additional income, stick to your plan and use the extra money to start paying down your debts. Here's a key to making this plan work: **Pay off your highest-interest debt first!** I have read many articles and books that speak of paying off your largest payments first, but I strongly disagree. The first debt you should pay off is the debt with the highest interest rate now or in the near future. Consider this scenario: Jasmine* has two credit cards with a total balance of $13,000 billed at an annual interest rate of 13.9 percent. Her minimum payment is $175. She also has a car loan balance of $28,000 at 3.9 percent interest and a monthly payment of $500 per month. If Jasmine is unable to refinance, consolidate, or reposition her assets to her advantage, then she needs to pay off the credit card first. The credit card has annual interest charge of

$1,807 per year and is more likely not to be a fixed rate, as compared to the car loan with annual interest payments of $1,092.

Another example would be if Jasmine had the same car in addition to a furniture loan of $13,000 at 0 percent for 6 months. First of all this is a NO-NO. If you cannot pay cash, don't do this loan! However, if it's already done, then work on paying off this loan first, because although it's at 0 percent now, it will go as high as 29 percent later - plus fees. These types of loans quickly and easily become unaffordable and unmanageable for individuals with limited funds. That's the reason those deals are so popular and so common; the companies realize that many of us will never pay them off, and they get rich while we struggle to pay for something that will be long gone before it's paid for. Again, use compound interest for good, not for evil.

---

**Meet Mr. Joe Public.**

Joe* has five credit cards with balances, a car loan, and a mortgage. Joe has budgeted $400 extra per month to pay off debt. He is applying $300 (75%) toward debt and saving $100 (25%) to pay himself and to prepare for future investment opportunities.

---

| Joe's Monthly Budget | | | |
|---|---|---|---|
| Credit Cards | Balance | Min Payment | Interest Rate |
| 1 | $ 17,500.00 | $ 357.00 | 19.9 |
| 2 | $ 8,900.00 | $ 255.00 | 7.9 |
| 3 | $ 12,253.00 | $ 295.00 | 11.9 |
| 4 | $ 3,900.00 | $ 105.00 | 21.9 |
| 5 | $ 895.00 | $ 145.00 | 11.9 |
| Mortgage | | | |
| 1 | $ 193,015.00 | $1700 PITI* | 5.5 |
| Car Loan | $ 18,060.00 | $ 427.00 | 5.9 |

*PITI stands for Principal, Interest, Taxes and Insurance*

**Joe's Debt-Reduction Plan:**
1. First, pay off the credit cards because they have the highest interest rates. The first credit card to pay off in this case would be credit card #4. However, if you have a financial obligation with a higher interest rate that can be paid off in less than three months, pay that first. Pay off credit card #5 because it has the lowest balance.
2. Next, once credit card #5 is paid off, focus on paying off credit card #4. Now that you do not have to make that extra $145 payment for the previous card, move up to 75% of that payment to credit card #4 and save the difference. For example, let's say that you paid the $895 balance in 3 months (approximately $300 per month). Take 75% of the new savings ($225) and add that toward the minimum payment on credit card #4.
3. Now Joe is paying $630 ($225+105+300) toward credit card #4. Joe is also now saving $175 ($100 + $75) per month which will help build a solid emergency reserve fund and plant the seeds for a good retirement and future nest egg.
4. Joe will continue this process over and over again until he is debt free. Learn from this example and incorporate it into your own debt-reduction strategy. Not only will you be debt-free, but you will have acquired the knowledge to prevent yourself and others from getting into the same situation again.

*Get Outside Help* – On occasion there are situations where there just isn't enough money coming in or accessible in savings. Some people will need additional help. I once heard a popular motivational speaker say, "It's OK to ask for help. But don't stop asking until you get it." That applies to your finances as well as life in general. There are many reputable credit counseling agencies out there to help consumers who find themselves in financial trouble. These agencies have counselors trained in budgeting, credit, and debt management. A good counselor should give you a personalized plan to help resolve your debt problems. Word to the wise, beware of so-called "credit repair" firms. In most cases, these companies are scams developed with the goal of separating you from your money. You can actually contact all three major credit reporting agencies on your own to correct anything that may be inaccurate or out of date, and there is no cost to do so. Contact information for all three credit agencies (Equifax, Experian and TransUnion) is located at the end of this book.

For as many reputable organizations as there are to help you, there are twice as many most likely out to get you. So, be careful and make sure you do your research before signing any contract, giving power-of-attorney to anyone to make legal and financial decisions on your behalf, and before paying any up-front "processing" or filing fees. Unfortunately, there are many "imposters" and "shiny suits" out there waiting to take advantage of your situation, so proceed with caution.

The National Foundation for Credit Counseling may be a good start. Also, your credit card companies can give you a list of other credit counseling firms they approve and may already have affiliations with. They can refer you to an agency that sets up a Debt Management Plan. This is where you pay the counseling agency and they pay your creditors for you in exchange for reduced rates and balances. Again, be careful. This is not for everyone, so make sure you weigh all your options against the severity of your situation.

In addition to companies that establish Debt Management Plans, some companies work on your behalf to negotiate settlements for a fee. These plans can be very risky because there is often an up-front fee before you get any results and they potentially can have a negative impact on your credit. As mentioned earlier, the best option is to avoid these people and try to settle with your creditors on your own. Use a firm like this as a last resort if you have an extremely high balance that carries high interest, and you've exhausted all other reasonable options. Something else to keep in mind also is that any form of debt forgiveness may be considered income by the IRS – which you then may be taxed on. You can find out details from a tax professional.

*The Last Resort* - Even though bankruptcy laws have changed in the past few years and filing for bankruptcy isn't as easy as it used to be, some people still use it as a "get out of jail free" card to avoid facing up to their responsibilities. Although there certainly are dire financial situations worthy of a bankruptcy option, this should be used only as a last resort due to the extensive damage it does to your credit report and the extended amount of time that the filing follows your credit history.

**Bankruptcy**- This filing is a legal declaration of the inability of an individual or organization to pay their creditors. It is a process in which consumers and businesses can eliminate and repay some or all of their debts

through a federal bankruptcy court. There are two primary categories of personal bankruptcy filings:
- Chapter 7 Bankruptcy- Known as "liquidation," it effectively erases all your unsecured debts. With the exception of "exempt" property, other assets you own such as your car, home, art, or jewelry may be used to pay off creditors. Chapter 7 bankruptcy remains on your credit history for 10 years. Not everyone qualifies for Chapter 7. If you have a regular income stream that exceeds certain limits then you may have to file Chapter 13.
- Chapter 13 Bankruptcy- Known as "wage earner," this option allows you to repay your debts over a 3 to 5-year period. This type of bankruptcy filing stays on your credit history for 7 years. Check www.usdoj.gov/ust for more information on the U.S. Trustee program which handles bankruptcy proceedings.

> $$$ Avoid the "credit crunch." Use credit, credit cards, and credit lines as a resource, not as emergency reserve funds.

Now is a very good time to get your credit card house in order. While credit limits are decreasing and everyone is feeling the pinch, you can use this window of opportunity to pay off debts, rebuild credit, and be in a position to take advantage of lower interest rates when the market begins to rebound and the credit squeeze begins to loosen its grip. In building or restoring credit, the goal should not be to have no credit at all, but rather to use your credit wisely. Use credit as a resource, not as an emergency reserve fund. Credit not only affects your purchasing power but it can affect getting a new job or getting life insurance to protect your loved ones. The goal is to achieve a high credit score of 720 or above. There are several easy ways to help build up your score.

1. Pay your bills on time. Make sure you follow your budget and make timely payments every month or however often your payment plan requires. In order: God first; pay yourself second through savings or investments; then pay creditors. Even when you slow pay (pay late but before 30 days past due), it still reflects a negative image to your creditors. **You want to be able to have more credit than you will ever need,** and paying bills on time helps accomplish this goal.

2. Start early on obtaining credit. I know that this sounds backwards, but it's true. The longer you have a credit history the better your record. Even after you pay off your credit cards, keep the oldest accounts open, because the longevity of credit history helps improve your score.

3. Keep the credit lines with the largest limits open. If you have a HELOC (Home Equity Line of Credit) with a $0 balance, don't close it, keep it open because it helps your score. Creditors look to see how you handle having credit, and if everything you have is "maxed out" then it makes them feel you are in a crunch and either they will deny credit or they will approve you with less favorable terms.

4. Don't have more than four revolving lines of credit (credit cards). Keep open the accounts that you've had the longest and that have the highest limits. I am not a fan of store credit cards because they do not have high limits and they tend to lower your credit score. Stick with Visa, MasterCard, Discover, and American Express.

5. Pay off your credit balance every month. Not only can this improve your score and help rack up those reward points, but it also puts the creditor at ease and gives them a reason to raise your credit limit which helps your score.

6. Limit your credit applications. Numerous inquiries on your credit hurt your score. For example, when you are shopping for a mortgage, find out the best terms from your lender in advance. Only when you are ready to proceed should you commit to a credit inquiry.

7. Check your credit at least once a year. The federal government allows consumers a free yearly free credit report. Visit www.annualcreditreport.com to request a copy. The website gives consumers access to receive a free credit file disclosure (not a credit score) once every 12 months from each of the three nationwide consumer credit reporting companies (Equifax, Experian, and TransUnion).

**Save, Save, Save...**

To save is one thing, but to save properly is another. There are several aspects to proper saving. Remember, first you systematically give God your tithe through your local church or ministry; next, pay yourself (savings and investments); and then pay all your creditors and bills. Making saving a core principle in your financial plan is crucial to achieving your goals. Take note of the following information to save for the present and future.

a. Save for your emergency reserve. This is the foundation of your savings plan. If you are single or if you have only one income in the household, then 12 months of expenses is an adequate amount. If you are married and have two incomes in the household, then 6 months is adequate. I know that you probably have heard to acquire 3 to 6 months of living expenses, but when the world changes, we have to change with it. Because of the lack of credit that is currently available, our country's uncertain financial future, and companies' reluctance to hire employees and give raises, now more than ever, it is important to save extra money… just in case. In other words, hope for the best, but plan for the worst. Saving this amount of money brings a sense of freedom and security to allow other things to happen in your life. I know it may seem impossible at first, but it's not. It may take you several months or years, but the important thing is to start as soon as possible.

Get in the habit of saving systematically. As soon as you get paid, you should have your savings debited right out of your checking account into a savings account. If you are paid twice per month, consider choosing the $5^{th}$ and $20^{th}$ of each month for your savings amount to go directly from your checking to your savings account. I have met with many people who were surprised that they were able to save so much money in their retirement accounts. In many cases, it is the largest account they have because money was saved every pay period and taken out of every check **systematically**. No, it's not necessarily going to be easy, but it is going to be worth it.

b. Saving for your retirement is important. We will discuss a lot more on this important topic later (See Chapter 11, *Planning for Retirement*); however, it is important to also save systematically for retirement as well.

c. Saving for your children's college education is crucial to your future peace of mind. Keep in mind that saving for college comes only after you have accumulated your emergency reserve fund, and you're on course for your retirement. Think about the last time you took a flight and what you heard during the flight attendant's instructions: He or she said, "In case of emergency, if we lose cabin pressure, your oxygen mask will automatically deploy from the compartment above. If you are traveling with small children, put on your oxygen mask first, then assist the child." I thought about that statement, and at first it seemed backwards - but it's not. You have to be steady, in control, and in good shape in order to sufficiently help someone else. The same is true with your finances. Many clients have come into my office with pre-existing college education savings plans which were very impressive on paper; only to have to pay a penalty or fee for taking out some of the funds to cover an unexpected emergency. Saving for college is important when done in its proper place at the appropriate stage of your financial plan. Here's how and why college savings can be a benefit:

*College Makes Sense* - Statistically, the numbers are staggering on how much more people with college degrees earn versus individuals who only earn a high school diploma. According to the U.S. Census Bureau, workers over age 18 with a bachelor's degree earn an average of $51,206 a year, while those with a high school diploma earn $27,915. Workers with an advanced degree make an average of $74,602, and those without a high school diploma average $18,734.

*Increasing Costs* - In recent years, college costs have increased more than the general rate of inflation (cost of living). On average, it will cost **$20,583** per year for in-state tuition to attend a public, state-funded university. However, if you have a child that is 3-years-old today, it is going to cost **$45,951** per year by the time that child is ready to attend (year 2025 with an average inflation rate 5.5 percent).

*Years of Study* - In the past, four years of higher education was more than enough, but that is no longer the case. Now many professions and degree programs require six or more years of study. Although there are many types of scholarships and fellowships available for professional degree programs, they are not a guarantee, so it is important to plan for additional expenses to cover tuition, books, and fees for each extra year of school.

## Ways to save for College - There are several tax-advantaged ways to save:

Of all the available options, I think that most people should invest in 529 plans. They are tax-advantaged and tend to have more investment opportunities than other college savings plans. It is highly recommended to incorporate investment options that allow for compound growth as part of your college savings plan.

*529 College Savings Plans* - These are state-sponsored plans that either allow one to prepay for college tuition or to contribute to a savings account established to pay for the student's "qualified higher education expenses." Contributions are not federally tax-deductible (although some states allow state tax deductibility), but they do grow tax deferred. If certain requirements are met, then the distributions used for "qualified higher education expenses" are excluded from income. Keep in mind that the fees, expenses, and features vary from state to state. Here are some additional benefits of the 529 College Savings Plan:

- Money is invested with after-tax dollars, and the funds

grow under a tax-deferred status as long as they are used for "qualified education expenses."
- Contribution limits are very high versus other college savings plans.
- Since donations to the 529 Plan are considered gifts, each donor receives a federal gift tax exemption ($13,000 in 2010); and a married couple counts as two donors with the ability to give up to $26,000.
- Plan allows for lump sum contributions up to $65,000 per individual or $130,000 per married couple for five years.
- Parents control the funds even after the child reaches the age of maturity.
- You can change beneficiaries of the plan. For example, if an older sibling gets a scholarship, you can change the beneficiary to another child and use the money for their education instead.
- Like any investment fund, there are risks, but the 529 Plan benefits outweigh most of them. Consult your local and state laws and seek the advice of a professional financial planner to learn more about this investment plan.

*Additional College Savings Plans*
- Coverdell Education Savings Account - Although it is not widely used anymore, this plan allows you to save $2,000 per year through year 2011. The money is not tax-deductible, but it is tax deferred. Many of the tax benefits in this plan are set to expire in 2011, mainly because of the popularity of the 529 Plan.
- U.S. Saving Bonds - Because savings bonds are issued by the federal government, they are exempt from state and local taxes. In addition, the interest earned on bonds can be tax-deferred until the bond is redeemed. Savings bonds are financial securities backed by the full faith and credit of the United States government.
- Uniform Transfers to Minors Act - UTMA accounts are generally used as custodial accounts to transfer ownership of cash and other financial assets to children who are too young to handle such assets. I see this mainly used when a minor acquires assets provided through some type of inheritance

(e.g. when one or both parents pass away and name the child as beneficiary).

We recognize that everyone will not be able to take advantage of these tax-advantaged college savings investment options. However, the lack of funding and advanced planning should not entirely derail plans to secure a quality education. If a scholarship or college savings and investment plan isn't feasible, then student loans might be the answer.

*Student Loans* - Always apply for federal loans, not private loans, because they offer much more flexibility. There are many college graduates that cannot immediately find work after graduation, and federal loan programs will provide a deferment in payments while individuals search for employment. Private loans tend not to be as flexible. In addition, the interest rates for federal loans tend to be dramatically lower than private loans.

The strategies we've discussed in this chapter are designed to help you manage your cash flow, reduce debt, control spending, save for emergencies, save for college, and invest for your future. It seems that everyone understands the importance of managing credit, raising credit scores, and getting out of debt. But there seems to be a lack of understanding when it comes to investing; and how much potential—and *opportunity cost*—is lost when we don't invest. Of course, there are no guarantees, but consider this example:

If you invested in a money market account for six years ($500 at 1 percent interest), it doesn't sound like a lot of money accrued - even with the benefit of compound interest. However, those same funds in 2009 could have been used to purchase shares in Fifth Third bank for $1.10 each and then sold a year later for $12 per share. Now that same $30,000 would be worth more than $327,264. Better still, you would have only paid 15 percent in capital gains taxes, thanks in part to what's known as the Bush tax cuts (for the wealthy). No, this scenario doesn't play out every day, but it's a good example of how having savings and investment plans—and following them—can pay off handsomely.

## The Power of Compound Interest

When it comes to money, think of it in terms that every decision you make in life is also an economic decision that can inflate or deflate your financial future. In the world of finance, it is often said that the greatest invention in mankind is compound interest, which is the interest calculated on both the principal and the accrued interest of an investment.

Compound interest means that each time interest is paid, it is added to or compounded into the principal amount and thereafter earns interest also. The ability to have your assets actually work for you is amazing. One of many lessons we can all learn from wealthy individuals is how to stop working for money, and let our money work for us.

I worked for a big financial services firm before I started Worth Financial. Next door there was a very successful mortgage company. I remember the senior broker/owner telling me that he made about $400,000-$500,000 per year in profit. We talked from time to time, and he said he would use our firm's services to do some financial planning, but he never did.

One day we were having a conversation, and I remember he told me that he would never have a car note; rather, he would always borrow against his home. So he bought expensive cars by taking equity out of his home. In actuality, by doing this, he was unfortunately financing his car for 30 years. So instead of paying $84,153 ($60,000 purchase at 7% for 5 years—which is high enough), he ended up paying $456,735 ($60,000 at 7% for 30 years)! When I saw him a few years later, he informed me that he had closed the mortgage company and filed for bankruptcy because he didn't save enough money and had taken on too much debt. It's no surprise that the story ends that way because that is one of the familiar traps many people fall into without a solid financial plan. Personally, I don't want anyone else to go through a situation like that. The key to unlocking the door of compound interest is to use it for good and not for evil (i.e., building a solid investment portfolio versus pouring money down the drain of depreciable goods). See the chart below to understand how substantially compound interest can affect your financial planning and investment strategies.

**Compound Interest and Savings**

| Initial Investment | Annual % Rate | Investment Term | Financial Return |
|---|---|---|---|
| $25,000 | 3 percent | 10 years | $33,598 |
| $25,000 | 6 percent | 10 years | $44,771 |
| $25,000 | 11 percent | 10 years | $70,986 |

$$$ If you don't remember anything else about this section, learn the No. 1 Rule of Investing: Buy low, sell high, and use compound interest to your advantage!

Congratulations on making it through this section. Remember, there are no identical plans because *Your Financial Plan is Personal* to you and your family. It may be necessary to read this section a number of times to thoroughly grasp all the information contained, but getting this far in the book is a major accomplishment. You are now well on your way to walking down the road toward financial freedom.

## Chapter 10 – Invest in Yourself

'As a man thinketh, so is he.' The way you think about money determines how you spend, save, and invest money. If you're thinking wrong, most likely your actions will be wrong as well because behavior follows mindset. In Romans 12:2 (KJV), we're told, "And be not conformed to this world: but be ye **transformed by the renewing of your mind**, that ye may prove what is that good, and acceptable, and perfect will of God." So, if you want to change your life, change your situation, or change your ways, you must first make a decision to change your mind. When you invest in yourself, you invest in your future.

**Free Your Mind and the Rest Will Follow**

If you haven't had a lot of financial training, or you aren't familiar with various financial tools of the trade, then a lot of the rules, regulations, and information can seem absolutely overwhelming. Attempting to learn about the financial market on your own through trial and error is dangerous and can be costly as well. There are a lot of families that have worked hard and saved money, only to have nothing to show for it at the end because they weren't knowledge about financial investment opportunities because no one taught them. Unfortunately, a lot of times in the Christian community, we see people who are saved, love the Lord, pay their tithes and offerings, yet never seem to excel because they don't understand modern-day financial principles and don't know how to take advantage of the opportunities that exist.

[Glen] Growing up, I watched my grandparents work hard and save money all their lives, but still had very little by the time they retired. The reason is because they never learned how to invest their money and make it work and grow for them. As a result, they consistently lost buying power every year because their money didn't keep up with the rate of inflation. We must understand that knowledge is power. In this day and age, what you don't know can bankrupt you. We have the assurance from scripture that God loves us and wants nothing but the best for us, and saving/investing is a tool to help us acquire His best. It's important to understand that God wants us to prepare and plan for the future.

There are a lot of misconceptions about investing—especially within Christendom because there is not a lot of information that discusses godly financial wisdom. Unfortunately, many of us are at one extreme or the other. One argument says that Christians should be poor because poverty is a form of godliness. Fortunately, we've already dispelled that myth in the previous chapter. The other argument is that investing is a form of gambling and although it may offer huge financial returns, the trade-off is a diminished relationship with God and an ever-increasing focus on acquiring more money and material things. Again, we encourage all things in moderation. It is not God's will for His children to be broke and constantly in need, nor is it His desire for us to make money and possessions our idols. There is an obligation to be good financial stewards and to generate wealth that can be passed down to the next generation. To be clear, investing in the markets is not gambling. Without question, there is risk involved, but the odds are in your favor for long-term investors. The casinos in Las Vegas and Atlantic City are beautiful for a reason – because odds are that you are going to lose. Or as the saying goes in gambling, 'the House always wins.'

Proper investing allows you to purchase into tangible companies, products, and services that meet a real need or supply a demand. True investing correlates with the cycle of business and the production of goods and services, not a whim, lucky numbers, or a hunch. Even still, it is important to seek out qualified professionals to lessen the chances of losing in the market. And remember there are some strategies that allow you to participate in market gains, but not market losses (Index Annuity). Did you know that Federal Reserve Chairman Ben Bernanke has nearly all of his retirement dollars in annuities? Not a bad strategy. And if it is good enough for the chairman of the FED, then it might work for you as well.

When you invest in the stock market you are literally buying companies. The stronger and larger the company, the better the odds are for success. For example, we know Walmart probably will not be going away anytime soon. Also, investing allows you to participate in the collective brain trust of experts and access the experience of successful people. I often hear people say that because they didn't go to the "right" school or get in the "right" circles, they can't succeed on a higher level. That is not the case. Although you may not know John Bogle personally (Vanguard Funds Founder) and may not have his Ivy-league education, you can still invest in his Vanguard mutual funds and benefit from the company's expertise. Investing opens a whole new world!

The people who are most successful in life are those who envision the future-based version of themselves and use their present-day self to plan on achieving that goal. Our God is a God of vision, and not just for today. We can learn a lot from other people who are already where we want to be in life. We can pray to God to send us the right people to help guide us down the path to financial independence so that we don't get misled by wolves in Financial Shepherd clothing. If you desire to be wealthy, you have to purposely meet with professionals who are trained to work with wealthy individuals and who know how to grow and maintain wealth. Also, if you know someone who has amassed wealth the right way, don't let your pride get in the way of reaching out to them.

One thing that I have learned over the years is that everyone has different goals. I remember when I worked for a large financial services company, they wanted us to sell certain financial products to everyone—whether they needed them or not—and I just could not do it. It is important to have a plan that is tailored specifically for you and your family.

One great way to invest that's easy for newcomers consists of index mutual fund or exchange traded fund (ETF) investing. The broad indexes are proven over time to increase, and they are very inexpensive to buy. While many mutual funds have a cost (that you don't see) of 1% - 5%, you can link to a broad index (like S&P 500) for a fraction of that cost. And you can set a bill and have it come right out of your checking account. Although it fluctuates and goes up and down like most investments, over time they tend to go up more than down. There is no perfect investment, but we will talk about very suitable ones in Chapter 11, *Planning for Retirement*.

## Why Should You Invest?

Investing in your future is the equivalent of investing in yourself – and vice versa. Think of investing as creating multiple streams of income for your household and a process that does not require additional work from you. Instead, you are identifying profitable ways to make your money earn even more money. By applying the principle of financial leveraging and using the power of compound interest, investing allows your money to go to work for you and help fund your future goals and aspirations. Investments make dreams come true. Here are some basic questions to ask yourself and to discuss with your financial planner when you are considering investment strategies:

- *Why am I investing?*
- *Do I need current income or am I saving toward my future accumulation goals?*
- *When will the money I plan to invest be needed?*
- *How much risk am I willing to take; and am I a conservative investor or an aggressive investor?*
- *Can I lose all or part of my investment fund and not have my standard of living affected?*
- *Are income taxes a concern for me?*
- *Will my investments change my overall tax status?*
- *What is the current economic forecast?*
- *Do I have enough knowledge, information, and skill to make wise investment decisions?*
- *Do I have enough time to manage my investment portfolio?*
- *How much do I have to invest?*
- *Do I have a good investment plan or do I have access to a good financial planner?*

"If knowledge is power, then what you don't know can be devastating." Many of us hear important information every day, but we fail to retain it. Not only is it important to have knowledge, but it is also important to be aware of what you don't know – and then be willing to learn so that no one can take advantage of you or your financial situation. Below are basic introductions and descriptions of some of the most common investment channels that are readily available and easily accessible to most people:

*Real Estate* - Many people have made a lot of money and lost a lot of money because of real estate investments. This particular strategy allows the investor to direct funds into tangible commercial, residential, developmental or rental property, gaining a financial return (or loss) from the sale or rental of the respective property(s). This has been a long time-favored investment for those who seek tax benefits and a hedge against inflation.

*Stocks* (shares) - A stock represents a share of ownership in a company.

Stocks represent a claim on a company's assets and earnings. The more stock you own, the greater ownership you have in the company. You have either direct or indirect ownership. Direct ownership means you have shares of a particular company registered in your name. Indirect means you invest in a pool of funds (e.g. mutual funds). Buying an individual company gives you more access and control. It's important to note that many advisors are not licensed to sell stocks, and many of the ones that do don't really know what they are doing. Use caution when entering the stock market, and work with a professional that knows what he or she is doing. Although they carry a high level of risk, investing in stocks can have high-yielding, life-changing returns.

*Bonds* - Also called bills, notes, or debt obligations, bonds are a type of debt security similar to an IOU. When you purchase a bond, you are lending money to a government, municipality, corporation, federal agency, or other establishment known as an *issuer*.

Since you are a debtor, bonds, by definition, are less aggressive than stocks. If a company goes bankrupt, then bondholders are paid whatever comes from the liquidation. You can also have direct and indirect ownership in bonds. There are three different types of bonds:

- *U.S. Government Treasury Bonds* - These are direct obligations from the U.S. government. They are generally considered the safest bonds, which is why they have a lower return compared to other bonds. They are federally taxable, but generally not taxed on the state or local level.
- *Municipal Bonds* - These bonds are from state and local governments or municipalities. They are also considered relatively safe. These bonds are normally exempt from federal taxes and generally exempt from state and local taxes especially if you live in that jurisdiction. Many affluent investors buy these to save on taxes.
- *Corporate Bonds* - These are from obligations from corporations. The stronger the company (less risk) means generally lower returns (not in all cases). Corporate bonds historically pay higher returns than Treasury and Municipal Bonds. However, you must also keep in mind that these bonds are taxable both on the federal and maybe even on state and local levels.

*Options* - These instruments are for "accredited investors," so you should become one as soon as possible! Although they are fairly complicated, they can really help protect your financial planning process. If you are not familiar with these, find a good professional that can help you. Did you know that some people make money when the stock market goes down? They are utilizing options. Just remember that "covered call options" can help provide extra income, and "put options" allow you to make money and/or protect your gains if the market goes down.

*Mutual Funds-* They are designed to pool funds of many investors to achieve a common purpose. The money raised is then invested in accordance to underlying goals. Mutual funds provide:

- Professional Management using trained experts and researchers.
- Diversification which provides increased protection. Instead of having only one security, with all your financial eggs in one basket, you reduce your risk by spreading it over several securities. Many funds have 50, even 100+ holdings at any one time.
- Convenience that allows the "small investor" to participate in the opportunities related to many securities.

Like any investment, there are also risks in owning mutual funds. However, when you are building your foundation, mutual funds are a great place to start. You first can save in a Money Market Account (MMA) or Money Market Deposit Account (MMDA) sold at any reputable bank. Note that these are not the same as Money Market Mutual Funds (MMMF) which are not federally insured, but were widely considered safe until Lehman Brothers went bankrupt. After accumulating a 2-month reserve in this investment fund, you should begin to spread your money around to various other funds as part of your overall investment strategy for wealth creation.

When starting out, it is important to choose a good mutual fund family. Fund families have broad spectrums of investments that meet the temperaments of investors at various times. For instance bonds may be the way to go if the stock market appears to be going downward. You should be able to move money into the bond fund without any cost. Remember, investing in mutual funds is a great place to start but not finish.

One of the professional guidelines I use when advising clients is based on a simple question I pose to myself: *"If this client was my mother, what would I tell her or him to do?"* More often than not, when I consider how I would advise someone close to me whose well-being is important to me, I find that Index Investing is often a good strategy that makes the introduction to investing painless.

*Index Investing* - This strategy is called "passive investing" because it is structured to follow the indexes such as the unmanaged S&P 500. There is no buying and selling, the fund just follows the index itself. "Active investing" includes all other mutual funds, and unit investment trusts, where there is a money manager buying and selling stocks to try and outperform the market. I am a fan of index investing for a couple of reasons:

- Lower cost- since there is no money manager buying and selling securities, the fund can't justify charging huge fees.
- Lower turnover- There is little buying and selling of securities, therefore there are few brokerage costs. In addition, when a security is sold, it triggers a capital gain. Since this is done drastically less than in "active" investing, it is more favorable for tax purposes.

It is likely that you haven't heard a lot about Index Investing because Wall Street doesn't promote it. The reason is that Wall Street does not make money by making you money; the investors on Wall Street make money by managing your money. Have you seen many commercials from Wall Street companies promoting their low-cost index funds? Of course not! They are not heavily promoted even though index funds generally out-perform actively managed funds. Many money managers typically live the "high life" and charge huge fees (that they hide in a prospectus that few people read or can understand) and investors simply accept lower returns. Even though we take on risk all the time, we only make money when the underlining securities in that fund go up. High-profile Wall Street investors get their fees regardless, so this is a good tool for you to become more familiar. Take time to study and review these different tools and strategies so that they become familiar and part of your financial vocabulary.

**Assess Your Investment Risk**

This part of the book is very dear to me because the information it contains caused me a lot of pain as a child; and this pain fueled me to find some answers. Years ago our family was in the process of losing our home, and my mother called her "advisor" to withdraw money out of her retirement account and my college savings plan so that we could pay to have somewhere to live. She was shocked to find out that there was little in the account because "Black Monday" (worldwide financial crash in 1987 when the stock market fell more than 22 percent in a four-hour period) happened just one week prior. Although she was risk adverse, the "advisor" still put her in what he thought was best. Since we basically were bankrupt, of course, we lost our home and the rest was history.

I felt helpless and I remember my mother feeling the same way. My goal as a financial planner is to prevent as many people as possible from experiencing a similar situation. After that, my mother never invested again. That one bad experience fueled a deep mistrust in the financial system and made her miss out on numerous opportunities to use the power of investing and compound interest for her benefit.

Truth be told, investing has changed my life and the lives of my clients for the better. My advice to you: Don't be afraid, be prepared! There is no such thing as the perfect investment so before starting to invest, you have to ask yourself some questions:

*Why are you investing?-* Do you need current income (i.e., bond interest or CD's) or are you saving for accumulation goals?

*When will the money be needed?* This is very important, because the sooner you need the money, the less aggressive you need to invest it. For instance, saving for a car you plan to buy next year should be invested less aggressively than your retirement funds that may not be needed for another 20 years.

*How much risk are you willing to undertake?* Can you lose all or part of your investment and it not affect how you live? We will talk more about this later, but most people don't really know what there risk tolerance is until they are faced with the situation. I remember in late 1990s (the biggest bull market of all time) so many people I met with said they were aggressive investors; that they were willing to deal with short- term losses in exchange for long-term gains. When the technology bubble burst, I saw them running away trying to sell, sell, sell! For that reason, I believe it is vital to have a **plan that changes** with the economy.

*Are income taxes a concern?* If the investment is taxable, will it change your overall tax status? This is important for everyone, especially high income earners. There have been people I met that made good gains in a year, but short-term capital gains raised their overall tax bracket and diminished the gains because of tax consequences.

*What is the economic outlook?* Investment strategies should be based on whether the economy is gaining or shrinking. This is very important to discuss. Just because you are an aggressive investor, doesn't mean you should stand idly by and watch your accounts crash when the economy is shrinking. That's like standing outside in the rain with a closed umbrella. You have the power to change your strategy and protect your assets.

Although a lot of this information may be new to you, it is certainly worth the time to expand your knowledge base and increase your options to build a solid foundation. Benjamin Franklin famously said, "If a man empties his purse into his head, no man can take it away from him. An investment in knowledge always pays the best interest."

Instead of viewing investing as a gamble or a whim, we should see it as a tool and gift from God to bless His people. This is one area where it makes sense to change our minds. Economist John Maynard Keynes said it best, "When the facts change, I change my mind. What do you do, sir?"

For starters, let's embrace the basic idea that the key to successful investing is to buy low and sell high. It sounds easy enough, but often our emotions and sometimes a lack of information keep us from achieving our goals. One of the first things to understand about investing is that you don't officially lose until you sell. If you buy a stock at $5 per share and it drops to $3, then you haven't lost yet because you're still in the game and there is a possibility that the price will go back up. However, if you sell, then your money is now out of the game and if it's in your savings account, you don't have the chance to make back your losses. It is important to know this from the beginning to help understand your risk level - that is how much loss you can tolerate without impacting your standard of living.

When you decide to start investing, another guiding factor to keep in mind is 'know thyself' because investing is a very personal process. Rarely do I find that two people think the exact same way about investing. In addition, how you feel today doesn't mean that you will feel the same tomorrow. As we grow older we tend to take fewer risks because our financial independence day is coming sooner than later. Also, things happen in our lives that change our thoughts and priorities and behaviors.

I remember in the late 1990s I had several new clients who said they were aggressive investors because they saw the stock market producing huge rates of return. Then after the technology bubble burst in 2000 and after the September 11th terrorist attacks when the markets fell, they had a change of heart and said they couldn't stand those types of losses. I witnessed many of them sell off and get out of the market, and they ended up losing most—if not all—of the previously earned profits.

Working with clients, I have found that in general, not only do we sell wrong, we also buy wrong. I've discovered that people (without real information) normally want to buy when the news is good. People tend to get excited when they hear everyone saying that a certain company has done well in the past and that it is poised to continue rapid growth. Of course, everyone wants to jump on board because it feels good. Well, by the time the news gets to you, you're typically buying too late, and it's just a matter of time before it starts to slow down or dip. The key to successful investing is to buy on discount, before the news is so great. That is what the pro's do, and by the time everyone else is hearing about the next big opportunity, they are out and on to the next big opportunity.

There are more than 8,700 publicly traded companies in the United States alone, so that means there are plentiful opportunities for investing all the time. The most profitable strategy is to buy a good company or fund that is positioned to go up, although it's down at the time. For example, when the banks hit hard times in the recession of 2008, nearly all the bank stocks dropped dramatically, although some of the stocks hit hard were still good stocks. They just paid the price of being hit hard because of the Lehman Brothers, Bear Stearns, Citibank's, etc... This was actually an excellent time to buy some of the smaller, stronger banks that were down only because the banking sector as a whole was down. I remember buying Fifth Third bank stock in February 2009 at $1.10 per share and selling it six months later for more than $8 per share. Granted, this does not happen everyday, but where there is crisis there is opportunity. Therefore the best time to buy is when everyone is nervous. I am not saying that you should buy just because a stock is low, because it may be a poorly run company, but if it is a good company, that is the time to snatch it up. Do your research, put your emotions aside, buy low and sell high.

It is hard for me to understand why Americans find the concept of buying low (without fanfare and excitement) so difficult. Truth be told, we practically break our necks to save a dollar or get a discount on every other type of purchase. Think about it: we clip coupons, drive an extra mile to save a penny on gas, wake up at 4:30 in the morning the day after Thanksgiving just to get the best sale. So why would we pay full retail price for stocks (buying when the news is good) and sell wholesale (selling when the news is bad)? The main culprit is emotion. When it comes to money—and parting ways with it—emotions cause us to make some really poor, illogical decisions. That's why it is good to have someone on your board of directors who you can trust not to be as emotionally tied to your money as you are.

**The Perfect Investment**

I am often asked how and where to find the perfect investment. I then ask my clients to define their idea of the "perfect investment," and this is what I typically hear:
1. Completely safe
2. 100% liquid
3. Tremendous gains every year
4. No income taxes due from gains

Yeah, right. As you may have figured by now, this simply does not exist. Therefore, we have to set parameters in our strategy so that we can achieve the highest results possible. When you invest you should look invest for three time horizons. We all have them and we should invest accordingly.

1. Short-Term (less than one year) investments have to be liquid. Examples include Savings/ Treasury Bonds/ Money Market Funds/ Conservative or Balanced Mutual Funds.
2. Mid-Term (one to 10 years) investments need to have some, but not total, liquidity. This includes saving for a dream vacation, new car, home maintenance, and other events that may happen within this time period. Consider Moderate Mutual Funds, Broad Based Index Funds (S&P 500), Dividend Paying Stocks, and High Credit Bonds/EIA Annuities.
3. Long-Term (10+ years) investments have low liquidity. The stock market (Index Investing) and EIA (Equity Index Investing) tend to work well in this space. This is primarily for retirement/ financial independence planning.

**Four Key Steps in Investing**
1. There must first be a budget in place. You have to make sure all the necessities (food, clothing, household expenses, and

taxes) are taken care of before investing. In addition you have to establish your emergency reserve.
2. Develop an investment plan.
    a. Set Investment Goals.
    b. Set Time Horizons: Short, Medium, and Long-term strategies.
    c. Determine Risk Tolerance for each time horizon.
3. Evaluate investment options.
4. Manage your portfolio by conducting periodic reviews.

Part of playing the investment game is knowing that you might lose money at some point. But that is why following God's financial plan works, because when we make His priorities our own, we are never losing money that we need to survive. Investment funds are separate from our standard operating budget for day-to-day living. Once we get paid, we honor God first with our tithes, then we set aside our investment budget to pay ourselves through saving and growing our funds, and we've either already paid off all debt, or have an effective debt-reduction plan in progress. This allows us to decrease debt and increase savings at the same time. This is an ideal financial management plan to avoid experiencing the highs and lows of investment roller coasters because you're worried about how much money you might lose and whether you'll be able to survive until the next paycheck. That is no way to live.

## Out With the Old, In With the New: 'Buy and Hold' No Longer Works

Growing up in Detroit, I had family and many clients who worked for General Motors. I remember how difficult it was to get them to sell their company stock. Many of them had worked there since the 1960s and 1970s which represented the 'good ole days' for Big Auto companies. Although GM returns have lagged for decades (compared to the S&P 500), and the company was having more problems than ever, GM loyalists held fast to the idea that GM stock would rebound.

Fast-forward a few decades, and we all know the outcome of that story. GM and many of its suppliers went bankrupt. The moral of the story: What is good today may not be good tomorrow. What goes up must come down. Hence, one key to investing is taking advantage of opportunities in our new economy that may be short-lived. Innovation brings change, and change happens every day.

## Learn the Lingo

Many times we hear that the market trades up 40 points or down 40 points on any given day. These comments reflect the importance of the overall stock market in determining the price behavior of individual stocks or bonds. Some experts feel that this is the key and major factor in determining the securities selection (buying or selling). They feel that the stock market is what matters most, not individual securities. Others feel that the individual company is the only factor when buying a security. Analyzing these various forces in the stock market is known as *technical analysis*.

We feel that studying the market is only one element in the security analysis process and it is helpful in making decisions.

For example, think about the fall of 2008. There were some companies that remained profitable and their outlooks remained bright. In fact, there were even a few banks that hardly felt the "financial meltdown." However, their stock prices still fell because the overall stock market fell. Therefore, it is important to watch the overall outlook of our economy; it's important to see the big picture and keep both short-term and long-term goals in mind.

There are many types of technical analyses available, but here is a list of the most common ones:

- Charting
- Market Volume
- Breadth of the Market
- Short Interest
- Odd Lot Trading*

I could write a book on technical analysis because of its profound effect on stock market determinations. However, we will cover that topic at another time – I just want you to be familiar with the term and its relevance to the industry.

Odd lot trading is a term that you need to know. As a matter of fact, the impact of this phrase is one of my motivations for writing this book. I remember early in my career speaking to a seasoned veteran Wall Street trader, and he told me he used odd lot trading as a way to diversify or sell a security all together.

Understand that many people and most institutional investors buy stocks in even lots (multiplies of 100). However, small investors may not be able to afford even lots so they but in lots smaller than that multiple - which are called "odd lots." For example, if you wanted to buy stock in

XYZ company, and it costs $203 per share, usually an investor would buy at least multiples of 100 shares; so let's say 500. That would cost ($203 x 500) $101,500 plus trading costs. But what if you wanted this stock and only had $2,000; then you could only buy nine shares ($1,827 + trading costs). That would be considered an odd lot trade which frequently works against small investors and puts them at a disadvantage.

Adding insult to injury, small investors are notoriously wrong in their timing of buying a security for a couple of reasons:
1. Small investors usually get crucial information last (too late).
2. They usually wait until the news is great before they buy.

Remember, when it comes to investing, the goal is to buy low and sell high. When the news is great, it's usually about something that has already happened – and that is too late. As a Financial Shepherd, your responsibility is to get in the game, learn the lingo, and stay in the game until you win.

As we said previously, what goes up must come down. Conversely, what goes down will also eventually come back up. Decades upon decades, we've seen that the market ultimately corrects itself – even in the face of huge trade and financial deficits and uncertain economic times. It is fairly certain that there will be more down days ahead, but when these days arrive, they open up huge opportunities to invest. The lesson I want you to remember is to keep saving so that you can invest like the professionals and take advantage of these good opportunities when they come along. When the market corrects itself, the pros win and win big – and you can too!

> $$$ In the world of investing, where there is crisis, there is opportunity.

## Chapter 11 – Planning for Retirement

**The Road to Financial Independence**

*The Bible does not give us any specific or technical details on retirement, but one thing is clear: God expects us to work and serve Him in all stages of our lives. Perhaps the benefit of retiring is being able to devote more time to serving God in a mission-oriented capacity and sharing His gospel with the world.*

Years ago, retirement was almost considered a time to die. Now it is considered the optimal time to live – and for much longer. According to the National Center of Health Statistics (2007 report), a child born in 1900 had a life span of 47.3 years versus a contemporary child born in 2007 now has an expected lifespan of 77.9 years. Therefore, many people in professional careers will live just as long in retirement as they did in the workforce. The question is: How will they survive?

Word to the wise, retirement should be a major consideration from the first day you enter the workforce—or as one colleague says—begin with the end in mind. In mapping out a strategy for retirement planning, be sure to ask (and answer) the following questions in conjunction with a financial planner who's qualified to advise you on various options for long-term retirement investment plans:

1. When do I want to retire?
2. What does retirement mean to me (full-time travel and leisure, part-time work, full-time volunteer/service/missions, etc.)
3. How much money do I need to fund my ideal retirement?
4. How will I pay for retirement?

5. How will I cover health care expenses or unexpected medical costs?
6. What is my lifestyle going to be like; will I increase or decrease my standard of living?
7. Where do I want to live? e.g., closer to family, in a warmer climate, or near specialty medical centers?
8. Do I want to keep my home, purchase my dream home, or downsize to something smaller and more economically feasible?
9. How would I like to manage the estate planning process to bequeath my possessions after I die?
10. What professionals do I have in place that can assist me with retirement and estate planning to accomplish my long-term financial goals?

As you think about how to answer these questions, keep in mind that there are three primary ways to pay for retirement:
1. Employer-based plans (retirement savings plans, company matching retirement funds, etc.)
2. Government-based plans (Social Security)
3. Personal plans (independent wealth, residual income, inheritance, etc.)

> $$$ Money Matters: To maximize savings and investment opportunities, take full advantage of employer-based matching retirement funds.

## The Need for Retirement Planning

For much of the 20th century, retirement in America was traditionally defined in terms of its relationship to participation in the active workforce. An individual would work full-time until a certain age, and then leave employment to spend a few years quietly rocking on the front porch. Declining health often made retirement short and unpleasant. Retirement planning, as such, typically focused on saving enough to guarantee minimal survival for a relatively brief period of time.

More recently, however, many individuals are beginning to recognize that for a number of reasons, this traditional view of retirement is no longer accurate. Some individuals, for example, are voluntarily choosing to retire early, in their 40s or 50s. Others, because they enjoy working, choose to remain employed well past the traditional retirement age of 65. And many retirees do more than just rock on the front porch. Retirement is now often defined by activities such as travel, returning to school, volunteer work, or the pursuit of favorite hobbies or sports.

However, this changed face of retirement—with all of its possibilities—does not happen automatically. Many of the issues associated with retirement, such as ill health, and the need to provide income, still exist. With proper planning, these needs can adequately be addressed. So, ask yourself, 'What exactly do I need and how much money will it take to comfortably retire?'

Retirement in the new millennium now encompasses many more complex issues than it did decades ago. When most of us were growing up, the terms Social Security and retirement were practically synonymous. The process was fairly straightforward: graduate from high school, maybe go to college, then get a job and stay there for 30 years while paying into the Social Security system; then retire, relax on a front porch swing, and collect a monthly payout in return for your years of dedicated service. Well, that is no longer the case, and complete reliance on an under-funded Social Security system that's heading toward bankruptcy is certainly a risky proposition. Here's why:

Social Security is a system of social insurance benefits available to all covered workers in the United States providing added protections against the societal pressures of advanced age, disability, and poverty. The program was initially launched in the mid- 1930s as part of President Franklin D. Roosevelt's New Deal package. The benefits are funded primarily by payroll taxes paid by covered employees, employers, and self-employed individuals, and they kick in at age 65 (or reduced benefits at age 62). The goal of Social Security has always been to provide a secure future for American workers. Ironically, that sense of "security" is slowly eroding because of an imbalance of more retired workers from the Baby Boomer generation receiving benefits from the system versus the number of current workers paying into the system. Additionally, economic downturn, decreased interest rate earnings, and escalating inflation rates have weakened the value of the dollar over time. It is quite possible that Social Security as we've known it for decades might no longer be in existence in the not-too-distant future. Successful financial planning for retirement will require an investment strategy much more comprehensive than Social Security – but at least it's a start.

To qualify for Social Security benefits, a worker must be either "fully" insured or "currently" insured. Eligibility for "insured" status is earned by acquiring credits based on wages or self-employment income during a year. In 2010, an individual had to earn $1,120 in covered earnings to receive one credit and $4,480 to earn the maximum of four credits for the year. Americans workers become fully insured by earning 40 credits or by working 10 years in covered employment. The following benefits are available for fully insured workers:

- Worker's benefit – Monthly income for a retired or disabled worker.
- Spouse's benefit – Monthly income for the spouse or former spouse of a retired or disabled worker.
- Widow(er)'s benefit – Monthly retirement income for the surviving spouse or former spouse of a deceased worker.
- Child's benefit – Monthly income for the dependent child of a deceased, disabled, or retired worker. The child must be under age 18; or 18 or 19 and a full-time elementary or high school student; or over 18 and disabled before age 22.
- Mother's or Father's benefit – Monthly income paid to a surviving spouse who is caring for a worker's dependent child who is under age 16 or over age 16, but disabled before age 22. If under age 62, the spouse of a retired worker receives the same benefits.
- Parent's benefit – Monthly income paid to the surviving dependent parent or dependent parents of a deceased worker.

Still, no matter how you look at it, the derived benefits from the Social Security system do not meet the ever-increasing costs of living and rising levels of inflation. Government-subsidized benefits alone are simply not going to be enough.

Another key consideration in retirement planning is medical and health care costs. Although there are several ways to fund medical expenses for retirees, such as out-of-pocket, former employer health insurance plans, and spousal insurance plans, in many instances, various aspects of coverage for Americans 65 or older are funded through Medicare.

Medicare is a social insurance program administered by the United States government, providing health insurance coverage to people who are aged 65 and over, or who meet other special criteria. Medicare has four parts: Part A is Hospital Insurance. Part B is Medical Insurance. Medicare Part D covers prescription drugs. Medicare Advantage plans, also known as Medicare Part C, are another way for beneficiaries to receive their Part A, B, and D benefits.

*What is a Retirement Package and What is Available to You?*

The last 25 years have seen dramatic shifts in the history of the American retirement marketplace. When the 401(k) plan was introduced in 1978, defined benefit plans (pension plans) were the primary type of retirement plan. Now, pension plans are almost extinct.

We've all heard the term 401(k), but what is it? The 401(k) is simply an employee contributory retirement plan. Contributions are completely discretionary. Each participant simply contributes to the plan their expressed (determined) percentage. These deposits are called *elective deferrals,* as each eligible participant has a choice to either receive the amount as income or defer receiving it and the income tax associated with the deferral. Unlike pension plans that forced employer contributions, employers are not required to contribute (match) in 401(k) plans.

Investing in 401(k)'s or other employee-sponsored retirement plans has significant advantages. The main one is the tax-deferred compounding growth of employee deferrals. The other one is the compounding effect of the employee match. **Ninety-nine percent of all workers should at least contribute the amount of the employee match.** Even if you are struggling, you cannot afford not to get the money you work so hard to earn.

For instance, if your company matches dollar for dollar up to 3 percent, then you need to contribute at least 3 percent. That's a 100 percent return on your investment before you even get started! *We show you in Chapter 10 how to accomplish this even if you are struggling to pay your bills.*

As we mentioned earlier, there are three sources for money toward financial independence (government, employer, you) and you can only count on yourself. The government will have a tough time just dealing with old entitlement issues, and most employers have already eliminated pension plans, passing the retirement burden from them to you; so again all you have is you.

If your company 401(k) does not have good active mutual funds (most do not) then look to see if there are index mutual fund options in your 401(k). If not, I encourage you to always invest up to the company match, then look elsewhere to invest the rest (IRA, etc.) Now more than ever, you must seize control of your assets and make decisions for yourself. No longer can you depend on your company to ensure a comfortable retirement. A Financial Shepherd understands this and takes advantage of the information, knowledge, and wisdom made available.

> $$$ Money Matters: After leaving your old job, always roll over your retirement to an IRA. An IRA gives you the option of investing your money the way that you want, versus being at the mercy of an employer.

Believe it or not, it is possible to invest too conservatively and undermine your overall plan for financial freedom. In numerous consultations with clients, I find that there are some people who simply don't want to take any risk at all. For them, the thought of losing what they have worked for far outweighs the opportunity for gains. Most people who follow this philosophy will not be able to reach financial independence, and the result is that they simultaneously retire from their jobs and their quality of life. You can cripple your chances of reaching financial independence by not earning enough.

As you read earlier there is no perfect investment, however, there is one that comes close, especially for people not willing to take much risk.

An Index Annuity is the answer because it allows investors to:
1. Participate in market growth through indices such as the S&P 500. You can link to the very indexes that most professional money managers can't beat.
2. Experience no loss of value due to a declining stock market.
3. Receive tax-deferred growth. This is an additional benefit for non-retirement accounts because they are already tax deferred.

The only thing that keeps this from being perfect is that it's not 100 percent liquid. However, for your nest egg, it is often more liquid than you will ever need because they typically provide at least 10 percent withdrawals annually. This means that you could spend your entire nest egg in 5-10 years. Who plans on doing that? No one! An Index Annuity is the ideal investment solution for even the most conservative investor.

> $$$ When you make the commitment to start investing for retirement, begin with the end in mind, and plan to stick with your long-term strategy.

The goal for retirement investing isn't just creating a magic number for the sake of having one. The goal is to produce an income stream that you can't and won't outlive – period! Once you have accumulated enough funds, it is important to preserve what you have. There are many types of investments that minimize risk and produce great income streams, and it's important to maximize the potential of any individual or employer-sponsored Qualified Retirement Plans that are already in place for you.

As a result of the recent economic downturn, many corporations have instituted cost-cutting and restructuring measures to reduce expenses, including offering early retirement packages. Common perks frequently included in early retirement packages include:

- Cash – a cash bonus, dispersed as a lump-sum or periodic monthly payments.
- Defined benefit pensions – retirement income rates can be adjusted to provide a higher pension benefit based upon years of service, retirement age, or percentage of the highest three-year earnings average.
- Defined contribution pensions – employers may allow retired workers to keep their funds in the company retirement plan. Benefits are based on a percentage of the annual salary and amount of money paid into the plan [e.g. 401(k) or 403(b) plans].
- Other benefits – other early retirement benefits packages may include group health or life insurance, job placement services, access to continued education opportunities, and retirement/financial planning expertise.

A retirement plan can be classified as "qualified" if it meets certain federal income tax standards. For the most part, employer or employee contributions to a qualified plan are tax-deductible and the earnings are tax-deferred until paid out of the plan. Employer-sponsored plans can be generally classified as either Defined Benefit or Defined Contribution. Defined Benefit plans specify the benefit amount a participant will receive at retirement, and Defined Contribution plans [401(k), 403(b) or SEP] typically set aside a percentage of salary income each year. The retirement benefit depends on the amount that has been contributed and paid into the fund. Other retirement funds include the traditional Individual Retirement Account (IRA) and the Roth IRA. Contributions to an IRA may be tax-deductible and the earnings grow tax-deferred, whereas contributions to a Roth IRA have tax-deferred growth, but are never tax-deductible. Speak with a financial planner to discuss the best option for you.

---

$$$ **Money Matters:** Never, never, never take out a loan against your 401(k) retirement savings plan. This is a very unwise move because it creates a scenario for double-taxation and lost retirement fund value.

*The Financial Shepherd*

In summary, Employer-Sponsored Retirement Plans are categorized as:

<u>Defined Contribution</u>
401(k)
403(b)
SEP IRA
Simple IRA

<u>Defined Benefit</u>
Traditional
Money Purchase
Cash Balance

<u>Other</u>
Employee Stock Ownership Plan (ESOP)
Profit Sharing

Other common choices for retirement savings, investments, and planning include:
- Savings Account
- Common Stock
- Bonds
- Real Estate
- Precious Metals


- Annuities
- Home Equity
- Continued (Part/Full-time) Employment
- Index Investing

A contemporary consideration for modern-day retirement planning is the idea of *longevity risk*. Due to longer life expectancies and advances in modern medicine, people are living longer than ever. In some instances, they are outliving benefits designed to help them survive and thrive during retirement. Corporate re-structuring has resulted in fewer employer-matched investment funds and fewer generous benefits packages. Many types of previously held financial entitlements are no longer in existence, and the burden of responsibility has shifted from employer to employee.

One of the biggest examples of the detrimental effects of longevity risk can be found within the Social Security system. For the first time in August 2010, Social Security paid out more in benefits than it took in, putting it on a precarious path to dismantle the lives and livelihoods of retirees all over the nation. The biggest lesson to learn from this example is that *you* are ultimately responsible for your own financial welfare. That is why it is important to keep God first in everything and continually seek Him as your source. "But seek first the kingdom of God and his righteousness, and all these things will be added to you," (Matthew 6:33 ESV).

Furthermore, no matter how young or old you are when you start the planning process, you must not leave your future up to chance or rely solely on the goodwill and generosity of others. A secure retirement does not consist of a plan based solely on:

<u>Adult children</u> – who may or may not be willing or able to financially assist or properly care for you as you advance in age;

<u>Social Security</u> – a government fund which may or may not still be around and able to reliably pay out worker benefits due to the increasing number of dependent retirees, economic recession, and inflation costs;

<u>Winning the lottery</u> – a one-in-a-million shot in the dark at best, which the Bible speaks against as gambling. It also encourages gain from others' loss and is contrary to the clearly stated scriptures about work, labor, and reward.

The best advice we can share is to keep your options open when considering the best avenues for retirement planning. As we've previously mentioned, Index Investing (see Chapter 9 – *Your Financial Plan is Personal*) is a powerful way of investing for a retirement fund. History books and online search engines will clearly demonstrate that over time Index Investing clearly out-performs most money manager accounts. The reason more attention isn't given to this type of investment fund is because it isn't profitable for the money managers on Wall Street. Because Index Investing just follows an index (such as the S&P 500), there is no need for high-dollar money managers to buy or sell stock. Of course, mutual funds and active money management serve a purpose for more aggressive growth with a higher risk tolerance; however, for long-term retirement planning and nest-egg building, Index Investing is a very good option.

## Financing Your Future

If you plan to be financially independent, then you must plan to never run out of money, meaning that you have money left over (after you've met all your own financial obligations) that is passed on to family, friends, church and/or charity.

The key in making this plan successful is starting today – right now if you haven't already. It doesn't matter if you are 21 and just starting out in your career or 55 and well into your career and had a few bumps in the road. Take action now because you will never get this day back again!

The goal for funding an enjoyable retirement is wealth creation and wealth accumulation. Part of that process is paying down debt and the elimination of all bad debts. The other part is having more than enough income to cover all your expenses and unexpected emergencies. The final phase is growing the value of the funds you have acquired for retirement purposes, hence allowing your money to work for you. As you approach retirement, ideally, you should not have any credit card debts, other unsecured debts, auto loans, or any other types of revolving credit debt looming overhead. In a perfect world, you don't want to still have a mortgage payment either, but that step may take a while to achieve. Although many people have a goal of paying off their home, this should only be a priority if the proper financial resources are in place. In the big picture, it makes more sense to put that extra money towards savings versus paying off the mortgage.

Speaking of mortgages, your housing decision is so important. To downsize or not to downsize… that is the question. Well, approaching retirement age, it usually makes sense to downsize for three major reasons:
1. Your home is now too big because the kids have grown up and moved out.
2. A spouse has passed away and now you are suddenly single.
3. You need to save some money and want something less expensive and more manageable.

Before making a major decision such as selling your home, be sure to check the market value of your home, then make sure that you can find something comfortable that is going to be less expensive. One extra point would be to remember that although you may pay less for a new, smaller home, it is vitally important to make sure there aren't exorbitant hidden repair costs and maintenance fees. There have been many instances of people purchasing smaller, fixer-uppers, only to spend more money than they save making repairs. Although it appears to be a savings in the beginning, it ends up being a loss in the end.

Modern-day retirement has taken on a whole new meaning, and it is an ideal time to fulfill personal goals and lifelong dreams. Poor planning or lack of finances should not be obstacles in your golden years. Retirement should be an opportunity to enjoy family, friends, and the fruits of your labor; not to experience a whole new group of worries and anxieties that will keep you up at night. The best way to ensure that retirement is a time of pleasure and enjoyment is to make sure you put a solid plan in place – as far in advance as possible – and follow it toward financial freedom.

> **$$$ Money Matters:** The goal for retirement is to create a comfortable income that you cannot outlive.

# Chapter 12 – Life Has Its Challenges, Be Prepared

[Sy] Sometimes bad things happen to good people. And oftentimes there isn't anything we can do about it. Some people face unexpected challenges head-on with faith, strength, character, and determination, while others simply run away or bury their heads in the sand. But as we all can attest, ignoring problems does not make them go away.

When we choose to ignore something, we make a conscious effort to deny that which is real. Although we pretend that "all is well," we are fully aware of the severity of the situation, its effects on our lives, as well as its consequences for ourselves and loved ones. One of the most commonly used defense mechanisms is denial. According to content on www.psychpage.com: "It is simply the refusal to acknowledge what has, is, or will happen." Denial is often associated with a painful event or circumstance that may be difficult to address. For example, I have a client, Monica*, who I have been counseling for three and a half months. Monica has been a widow for the past two years and recently allowed her 23-year-old son to move back into her home. Her son currently does not contribute to any of Monica's financial obligations, and as a result of poor planning and misuse of her resources, Monica is only days away from foreclosure on her home of 17 years. When I asked Monica about her plans, she responded, "God will take care of it." I asked her more specifically, "What will God take care of?" She responded, "He will take care of my house note." So I delicately asked Monica, "Do you think that God is responsible for you facing the possible loss of your home?" Regardless of Monica's response, she obviously is in denial of what is really going on. But she is not alone.

Taking into consideration that Monica is still dealing with some complicated issues of grief associated with the loss of her husband of 28 years, it is much easier for her to create this fantasy as though her financial woes do not really exist. Shifting the burden of responsibility solely onto God allows her to relinquish her end of the bargain – but not really. The Bible itself doesn't support such action, which is why we read that 'faith without works is dead.' It is naïve to think that we can merely speak words of faith without any supportive action and expect financial miracles to fall out of the sky. Yes, God can take care of your mortgage by blessing the work of your hands to save, invest, and pay your bills on time. But let's be clear, the "work" is a requirement.

The reality is that Monica, like all of us, will have to face challenges that seem to consume our very existence at the time that we are experiencing them. And though God is able to do far more than we can ask or think, the question is: 'Did we seek Him prior to making the decision that put us in this predicament to begin with?' Like it or not, choices have consequences.

Every problem we could potentially face has a solution, but it is up to us to look to our heavenly Father, who is the author and finisher of our faith, for the answers that we need.

Proverbs 16:3- *Commit your work to the LORD, and your plans will be established.* [ESV]

Proverbs 21: 5- *The plans of the diligent lead surely to abundance, but everyone who is hasty comes only to poverty.* [ESV]

Proverbs 21:20-21- *Precious treasure and oil are in a wise man's dwelling, but a foolish man devours it. Whoever pursues righteousness and kindness will find life, righteousness and honor.* [ESV]

Matthew 12:25- *Knowing their thoughts, he said to them, "Every kingdom divided against itself is laid waste, and no city or house divided against itself will stand."* [ESV]

Philippians 2:3, 4- *Do nothing from rivalry or conceit, but in humility count others more significant than yourselves. Let each of you look not only to his own interests, but also to the interests of others.* [ESV]

James 1:5- *If any of you lacks wisdom, let him ask God, who gives generously to all without reproach, and it will be given him.* [ESV]

### [Glen] The Good, The Bad, The Ugly…

First, the bad news: Sometimes there are people you just cannot help because they aren't ready to be helped; and no matter how much you want something for someone else, you cannot do it for them. Change has to start with the individual who wants to change. I have a client who was known as one of the most prominent professionals in the city. He and his wife wore only the best clothing. In fact, he would frequently fly overseas just to meet with a tailor. They drove brand new, luxury cars and lived in a mansion. Their children attended the most expensive private school in the city and lacked for nothing. They had luxury box suites for all the major sports teams in the city and threw the best after-parties around town. Without question, they were the "it" couple and quite the talk of the town. Most people figured them to be one of the wealthiest and most prominent couples in the entire state.

Here's what people didn't know. This couple had a dirty, little secret. They spent practically every dollar and cent they earned just to keep up appearances and impress the people around them. Yes, they were rich, but not wealthy. There is a huge difference between the two. The husband made several million dollars per year, but they spent almost all of it on things that would give them temporary enjoyment and a higher social status in the community. The couple had very little savings in comparison to their income. When legislation changed and earnings decreased, they were almost immediately bankrupt. Unfortunately, the threat of financial disaster wasn't enough to persuade them to change their ways because they were more interested in appearing to be rich than actually taking steps to build wealth.

When this couple was referred to me, one of our first tasks was to go through their budget line by line to identify wasteful spending and implement cost-cutting measures. Despite the fact that they were in way over their heads and practically drowning in debt, their initial reaction was resistance – because they were concerned about what other people might think if they no longer lived an extravagant life. My advice to them—as it is to you—is that as children of God, you have an obligation to be good stewards over the things that God has blessed you with, and it's your responsibility as Financial Shepherds to demonstrate godly principles with your finances. Ultimately, they had to make tough decisions like letting go of the luxury suite at the football stadium, purchasing clothing from a less expensive tailor here in the United States, and even buying used cars instead of trading new ones in every year or two for a newer model. It literally took several years to dig them out of the financial hole they were in and get them to a point of financial stability, but now they are on track and better prepared for future challenges to come.

Now, the better news: I find that there are many families that are stable with good employment, savings, and low debt levels - but who still demonstrate poor financial planning. This is one good reason to establish a *board of directors* and to be surrounded with other Financial Shepherds who support your life vision and want the best for you. One of the dangerous things about venturing into unknown territory is that you simply don't know what you don't know.

I've realized that pride is usually a big part of the reason why people do not ask for help when they need it. However, my perspective on seeking wise counsel is different. If the President of the United States—the most powerful position in the world—can humble himself enough to have a Cabinet, then why don't we? For instance, he has the Secretary of Defense because he realizes that he does not know everything about defense; the same with commerce, education, and economics. People in stable families need to employ the same tactics. Remember there is an opportunity cost with every decision that you make, and it is important to know what that cost will be. Just because you're doing well, doesn't mean you can't do better. When you are blessed to be a blessing and have extra resources to share, it is possible to do good and do well at the same time.

The Bible tells us in Philippians 4:5 to do all things in moderation. From a financial standpoint, that scripture is meant to keep us from extremes of lack or excess. I have a client who told me that she had been taught to have zero debt; none. She paid cash for everything, had no credit card debt, and even paid off the mortgage of her first home in 10 years. On the surface, this sounds like a really good thing. Fast forward a few years, and she wanted to move to a more prestigious part of town and was wondering how to make this happen. Her thoughts were to sell her home and take all of the earnings and invest in her new home, then sign up for a 15-year mortgage to pay it off faster. All of this sounds great, except that she had a few holes in her plan.

First, she did not have an emergency reserve fund; she only had a line of credit on her home. She also has a son who was 10-years-old at the time and she had not saved anything toward his education. At age 45, she would have to work until age 70 before she could retire comfortably because she had not saved enough in her retirement to cover her living expenses. So I recommended some changes in her plan:

1. Save and invest. Put only 20 percent down on the new home and invest the difference. Her mortgage rate was 5 percent fixed for a 30-year loan (versus 4.75% for the 15-year, not including its deductible); and over the last 10 years the S&P 500 index has averaged over 8.5 percent.

2. Invest for the future. The payment difference between the 15- and

30-year mortgages was $900 per month. I recommended that she save that extra $900 to invest and help build a college savings fund for her son.

3. Earn rewards. She loved to travel, so I suggested she get a travel reward credit card and pay it off every month to get extra bonus travel points. She put everything on her credit card and paid it off every month and received multiple free airline tickets which saved her thousands of dollars per year simply by paying with a reward card. Just by taking some basic, straightforward steps, she was able to take a good financial situation and make it much better in addition to being much better prepared for the future.

Now, the best news: There are some people who just get it right. They read, study, listen, and learn everything they can about finances and then put that knowledge to work and allow the money they save and the power of compound interest to work wonders for them.

One client in particular comes to mind. He is single and has saved on his own for years. He earns approximately $150,000 per year and saves 50 percent of his income. At age 40, he already has amassed more than $1 million. He invested most of his money on his own by reading various books about the "buy and hold" strategy and diversification. However, when the market dropped in October 2008, he sold at the market's lowest point and didn't get back in the game. When we met to discuss his finances, he shared with me that he knew that he should not have sold, but emotionally he could not stomach that level of risk. Fortunately, he gave me permission to take over his investments, since I had no personal or emotional attachments to his money.

In March 2009, we noticed that the market was beginning to turn around, so we bought several investments on his behalf. When he received the online statement, he immediately called me to confirm that the information was accurate. It was. Six months later his entire portfolio had increased by 400 percent under our management. While this clearly doesn't happen everyday, listening and learning from others can certainly help. When you build your financial future on a solid foundation, the potential is unlimited.

## A Plan for Every Season

Singles: Regardless of how you grew up, your life as a single adult is a great opportunity to start fresh and establish yourself as a successful Financial Shepherd. It may seem difficult to imagine yourself 10 or 15 years down the road when you're just starting out your career and embracing your newly-found independence. But now is the ideal time to get your financial house in order - without the added responsibilities of a spouse, in-laws, and typical marital obligations involved in running a household.

Take crucial steps now to build a board of directors, pay off debts, increase your credit score, open a savings account, and invest in a retirement fund to yield HUGE financial rewards in the future.

Engaged and Married Couples: The biggest mistake you can make is to wait until you are married to start talking about money. One of the most common issues that couples fight about is money, so it is vital that the channels of communication are open and cleared early. Interestingly enough, the intensity seems to increase when the woman earns more than the man. Usually, the issue revolves around insecure men who are not comfortable with their role in the relationship, causing a "power struggle" about who wears the pants in the relationship. Word to the wise, when it comes to finances and relationships, the best thing you can do is put your pride aside. The person with the better financial skills and knowledge is the person who should "wear the pants" (while the other person learns) and function as the Financial Shepherd of the family, leading by example and demonstrating the types of financial decisions that are best for the family. In particular, women need to make a special effort to learn about managing finances because they tend to have greater influence on household purchases and also statistically live longer than men and end up controlling the entire financial estate anyway.

The issue is not about who's in charge, because the goal of the marriage is for two individuals to become one; playing on the same team and working toward the same godly goals. During discussions about money, it is also important to start identifying key individuals who can serve on your board of directors. Make communicating about money a priority in your relationship so that it does not become an issue later on.

Single Again: Whether it is because of divorce or death, the loss of a spouse is a devastating event. Here is a guide from the *National Endowment for Financial Education* about steps to take to restore your stability and continue the wealth-building and financial planning process. Some people find it helpful to include trusted family, friends, and professionals when gathering information or materials. You may find it beneficial to ask someone to accompany you to take notes or provide emotional support as you tend to the following actions:

• If widowed, obtain at least 20 copies of your spouse's death certificate. It is usually easiest to request all the copies at once and keep them in a secure location to use as needed. Extra copies can be tucked away for future needs. You'll need to send this document to the Social Security Administration, credit card companies, your mortgage holder, and insurers to verify the death and either change the name on accounts or collect money that is due to you.

• When gathering professional advice, get sufficient information to enable you to make decisions that are right for you. Estate-planning attorneys, tax accountants, and financial advisors should have experience in helping widows and widowers deal with the particular circumstances of being newly single due to the death of a spouse. In addition to notes that you or a friend might take, ask these professionals to provide you with written summaries of meetings so that you can refer to these notes after your face-to-face meetings.

• Rename beneficiaries on all insurance policies, retirement accounts, and other accounts where your money is held.

• Update your will. In most states, the death of a spouse invalidates a previous will.

• Contact the Social Security Administration.

• Don't be pressured by others to make hasty financial decisions.

(*"Suddenly Single" – Financial Psychology and Lifechanging Events*, National Endowment for Financial Education, Greenwood Village, CO, 2004.)

## Documents You Need to Gather

For some people, organizing financial records is a dreaded activity, while others find it therapeutic to pull things together. Most people will need to take time to locate and organize the many important documents that are necessary for understanding the financial picture of the newly single. Whether you have lost your spouse through death or through divorce, you will need to locate these documents so that you can determine how much money you have to plan for current and future expenses. Allow yourself some time to heal emotionally from your loss and gain a better understanding of your financial picture before making major investment decisions. You may want to practice a response that you'll be comfortable with, such as "I appreciate your ideas and will take them into consideration when I'm ready to make those decisions."

*Records needed to assess your financial situation include:*
• Checking account statements

- Savings account statements
- Credit card information (including names under which the cards are listed)
- Retirement account information and statements (IRAs, 401(k)'s, Keogh, company pension plan, etc.)
- Employer stock option plans
- Mortgage payment record
- Deed to your home (or if renting, the lease agreement)
- Deeds to any other property
- Wills, living wills
- Powers of attorney
- Receipts for major purchases
- Warranties
- Car titles and registrations, with loan information or lease agreements

Widows and widowers usually are not faced with the same time pressure to gather this information as are couples undergoing separation or divorce proceedings. In separation or divorce situations, it is usually best to gather this information before one or the other partner physically leaves the marital home—potentially taking some of the information with them.

- Birth certificate
- Marriage certificate
- Copies of death certificate (if applicable)
- Tax returns
- Insurance policies (homeowner's, auto, health, life, disability, long-term care)
- Brokerage account statements
- Stock and bond certificates
- Mutual fund account statements
- Business partnership agreements
- Business buy-sell agreements
- Prenuptial or postnuptial agreements
- Social Security records
- Safe deposit box information (location and key)
- Trust agreements
- Pay stubs, along with current beneficiary designations of life insurance and pension/IRA accounts.

(*"Suddenly Single"* – *Financial Psychology and Lifechanging Events,*

National Endowment for Financial Education, Greenwood Village, CO, 2004.)

**Be Prepared**

Abraham Lincoln once said, "If I had eight hours to chop down a tree, I'd spend six sharpening my ax[e]." The point is that the will to prepare is as important as the will to succeed because success comes when preparation meets opportunity.

Our goal through this book is to prepare you for your future role as a Financial Shepherd and to help you gain the following characteristics:

a. *Confidence* - The ability to lead, and not just blindly follow; to finally feel refreshed and full of faith that your financial future will be better than it has ever been.

b. *Direction* - For many this will be the first time that you are fully aware of where you're going and how to get there. This financial map will provide direction and guidance and give instruction on how to navigate the hills and valleys that lead to success.

c. *New capabilities* - Many people cannot obtain wealth because they are unaware of all the blessings of God. Ignorance is no longer an excuse. Stocks, options, derivatives, and mutual funds are available to God's children to bless His people. It is time for us—that means you too—to openly receive this information and prosper. We believe that many millionaires will be created from reading this book.

---

$$$ Prepare your children to become responsible with money by training them early with piggy banks, interest-bearing savings accounts, children's books on financial literacy, basic allowances, and participation in family budgeting discussions.

# Chapter 13 – Hope for the Best, Plan for the Worst

More than all the others, this chapter brings up topics that no one really wants to talk about. 'Hope for the Best, Plan for the Worst' focuses on the sometimes random, yet inevitable events in life that occur (illness, disease, disability, death) but are never fun to discuss. As Christians, although we believe that there is a better life ahead in heaven, from the looks of things here, we don't necessarily live according to our beliefs. Many people become so selfish throughout their lives on earth that they don't properly prepare for dying, death, or leaving behind a positive legacy for others to follow and embrace.

Responsible planning is a significant part of our obligations as good stewards of God's gifts and also as Financial Shepherds setting a good example for others to follow.

It is of the utmost importance that we prepare ourselves and others (those that we leave behind) for the perils and hardships of life that often create financial difficulty if not addressed. Unfortunately, many of us find ourselves in a reactive mode instead of a proactive mode; responding to the latest crisis instead of simply implementing the plans that we have already put in place in advance. What's worse, when times are tough—such as in the current economic downturn—we tend not to follow our faith, but rather our sight and circumstances. In times like these, it is important to focus on the first principle of godly finances: everything belongs to God, and as long as we are obedient to His will, we will be blessed according to His Word, no matter what else may be going on around us.

## The Need for Responsible Planning

One of the most readily available and reliable types of financial planning comes in the form of Life Insurance. Historically utilized by the wealthy to ensure a comfortable standard of living for loved ones, the purchase of life insurance provides a sense of security and stability often included in wills and estate planning. Life insurance is a contract between the policy owner and the insurer, where the insurer agrees to pay a designated beneficiary a sum of money upon the occurrence of the insured individual's or individuals' death or other event, such as critical illness or terminal illness. In return, the policy owner agrees to pay a stipulated amount at regular intervals or in lump sums to maintain an active, executable policy.

Generally speaking, wealthy individuals tend to have a lot of life insurance, because for oftentimes minimal investments, the returns pay off quite handsomely. They also understand that life insurance policies offer one of the largest tax loopholes in the federal tax code. Just think about paying pennies on the dollar for a huge death benefit that goes to your family (normally) tax free. Also, the cash value inside the policy typically grows tax-deferred.

When meeting with prospective clients and discussing the topic of life insurance, there are two very common responses:

1. "I already have enough life insurance at work."

2. "I want just enough life insurance to pay off all the debts and (maybe) pay for the children's college education."

These responses, although common, are very dangerous because they put the individuals and the families they are obligated to care for in jeopardy in the event of a major medical or life-threatening crisis.

First, it is typically very inexpensive to buy policies at work which is always a plus, and many employers routinely pay for life insurance which is an even bigger plus. However, who do you know these days that stays at the same job for 30 years and then retires? Lately, that's a rare scenario. Your benefits package at one job will differ from another, so it is important to make sure you aren't relying on a defunct benefits package from a former employer to sustain your family's livelihood. Also consider what happens once you retire. Even if you have a nice retirement package at work, most places drop or slowly decrease and then eliminate your life insurance after you retire. You cannot solely count on your job to protect you. Think about retirees from General Motors and other large corporations hit hard by the recession. Not only are the current employees experiencing job losses, wage decreases, and a reduction in benefits, so are the people who were promised security, pensions, insurance, and retirement benefits. The economic and retirement expectations just aren't the same anymore, and it's a risky proposition to rely on someone else to have your best interest at the forefront of their priorities.

Second, yes it is important to pay down and pay off debts, but that is not the only thing to consider. In retirement and insurance planning, income replacement is often overlooked. If your previous lifestyle required two incomes for survival or to sustain the level of financial security you desired, how will you survive with just one income in the future? Also, inflation is an important factor to consider. As the cost of living goes up, buying power goes down. Therefore, you must not just think about today, but how much will your loved ones need to survive 20 years from now?

*There are three popular categories of life insurance:*

1. <u>Whole Life</u> – This type of insurance is also referred to as permanent insurance, or ordinary life insurance, and it is designed to stay in effect for the duration of your lifetime. As long as the policy owner meets his/her obligations under the policy, the policy remains in effect regardless of any changes in medical or health status. Throughout the duration of the whole life insurance policy, premium payment costs remain relatively stable, and a portion of each premium payment is set aside to earn interest. Over time, a whole life policy will develop a cash value and accumulated cash values form a reserve which allows the insurer to pay the policy's full death benefit.

2. <u>Universal Life (Traditional, Variable & Equity-Indexed)</u> –Universal Life Insurance is a variant of Whole Life Insurance in that it separates the mortality expense and cash value component of a policy. This method allows the insurance company to offer a higher degree of flexibility in the contract and also allows the policy owner to update or adapt the policy as needed based on changing lifestyle requirements or circumstances. These policies are unique in that they have several different provisions for which a policy holder may access the accumulated cash value without surrendering the policy or causing it to lapse.

3. <u>Term Life</u> – As the name suggests, "term life insurance" policies provide coverage for a limited period of time, or term. If there is no incident or death during the period that the policy covers, no benefits are paid out, and there is no refund of premiums paid. The policy provides only pure insurance protection and does not have the cash value feature typically found in most permanent life insurance policies.

Of the types of insurance policies available, term insurance is the cheapest. It is great when you are just starting out because you can buy a lot of insurance inexpensively. The drawback is that most people tend to outlive the term insurance because it is only there for a specific period or "term" of your life. If you start off buying term insurance, just make sure it is convertible to permanent insurance to achieve the maximum benefit.

Life insurance companies are managers of risk, so they know the odds are in their favor that you will not die or have a debilitating accident occur within that insured term policy time period, which is why the policies are so inexpensive. On the other hand, permanent policies like whole life (thus the name) and universal life are made to last your entire lifetime and pay out full benefits when the appropriate time arises. Many times, insurance companies may recommend or promote buying term insurance and investing the difference in mutual funds or stocks. Our advice is *buyer beware* because there are some major flaws in this strategy:

1. The first decade of the new millennium has shown all of us that the stock market can fall sharply and unexpectedly, so the premise behind investing the difference is based on the idea that you will have enough money to be self-insured after a period of time. But if the market falls and you lose half the value of the investment, then what will you do?

This particular strategy backfired on an older couple who gambled and loss by attempting to leverage a term insurance policy using the stock market as an anchor. The husband became ill and was denied the opportunity to purchase new or additional life insurance due to poor health conditions. The money from the original investment was lost, and the term period on the insurance policy expired, leaving the family without coverage. The end result is that the husband passed away and left the wife and other family members without enough money to meet basic expenses or maintain the quality of life to which they were accustomed. Situations like that are examples of why it's important to discuss your real financial situation, risk tolerance, and expectations with a financial planner and to create a customized plan that is tailored to your exact needs.

2. Life happens! Due to emergencies and rising costs for everything, occasionally there may be justifiable reasons why you have to use some of the money from your life insurance policy. Again, the risk is that you will no longer have enough money to take care of your loved ones because there isn't anything extra to invest. Adding insult to injury, as we grow older, life insurance becomes more and more expensive so when you try

to get more later, that once cheap term insurance might be unaffordable and out of reach.

Remember: All insurance companies and policies are not created equal. When searching for a policy most suitable for your needs, here's what you want to look for:

1. Quality of the company. There are three main rating agencies: A.M. Best, Standard & Poors, and Moody's. You want an insurance company that is rated A- or better. A company's guaranties are only as good as their strength to keep them. In addition, you (or your board of directors) should also review the company's financials. Companies that take less risk typically win the race. It is worth doing the research to make sure the insurance company you are considering is not on the brink of bankruptcy or about to go out of business all together.
2. Convertible term periods. Make sure any term policy you purchase is convertible to a permanent policy. It should have 10, 20, or 30-year options.

When meeting with your insurance agent and/or financial planner to discuss what type and how much life insurance to purchase, our recommendation is always to get as much as you can afford. High-paying policies can be used by surviving relatives to pay off a home mortgage, fund college educations, pay off debts or other loans, finance business transfers, cover medical bills, pay off death and estate taxes or other settlement costs, or create a new estate to be passed on to the next generation. Other things to consider in the planning process: a) Estate taxes; b) Education funds; c) Parents/Family members who need assistance; d) Charitable giving to church/ministry, etc.

As difficult as it is to talk about, think about, or plan for death, it is one of the necessities of a responsible life. But sometimes it isn't death that brings us to a halt, it's an unexpected accident or illness that literally knocks us off our feet. Here are more tools to help you plan for the worst:

**Disability Insurance**

Many people believe that their biggest asset is their home. For most of us, our biggest asset is the ability to work and earn an income. Not being able to work—due to job loss or a disability having taken away the ability to work—is often financially devastating.

Everyone who works for a living is very familiar with what can happen if they are fired. On the other hand, the possibility of becoming seriously disabled is a risk few seem to think much about. How likely is it that you will become disabled? According to one study, 30 percent of all Americans between the ages of 35 and 65 suffered a disability lasting at least 90 days. The risk of disability is real. The question is, 'What to do about it?'

Group Disability Insurance

Many employers will provide—or make available—disability insurance on a group basis. However, even those who are covered by a group policy can still be at substantial risk. Employer-sponsored disability policies seldom provide you with more than 60 percent of your monthly salary. Many policies set a monthly maximum benefit that may be far less than what some people earn. Income taxes can also be an issue; if the employer is paying the full cost of the coverage, disability benefits are fully taxable.

Individual Disability Income Insurance

For many, the real solution to the disability problem is individual disability income insurance. Although individual policies may cost you more, as long as you pay the premiums, the benefits are not taxable. Plus, an individual policy allows you to tailor its terms to fit your own needs. Factors to consider when shopping for an individual disability policy include:

-Company strength: You need to know if the company is financially sound.

-Definition of disability: Look for a policy that defines disability in the broadest terms possible. Some policies will permit you to work in a different occupation and still collect disability benefits.

-Elimination period: How long must you wait before disability payments begin?

-Benefit period: How long will you need coverage? Both short-term and long-term disability benefits are available.

-Inflation protection: Try to find a policy that adjusts benefits for inflation"

If you are **self-employed** or thinking of becoming self-employed, you have to think about more than just your family now. Factor in that your business is also a loved one. What happens if the business owner becomes disabled? What happens if the business owner dies?

While you are disabled, your business will fail unless you have proper planning in place like disability insurance to cover the monthly expenses and/or to pay for someone with your expertise to cover your job duties while you are out. Doctors hear this all the time in medical school, but most business owners do not think twice about properly insuring themselves.

Also, you have to think about the impact on the business if something happened to the key employees who are vital to the growth of the company. In the insurance business, these individuals are called "key persons." You may also want to consider additional life insurance for them to protect your company and their families in the event of an accidental injury that requires covering their responsibilities or replacing them. Women business owners definitely need to factor this in because statistically, women are more likely to have a disabling event occur than men.

Finally, another important policy to have in place is *long term care insurance*. If your employer offers it, then make sure it's transferable upon your departure to a new job or into retirement. We recommend that people start looking at this investment around the age 50 at the latest. Like any insurance, the younger you are the less expensive it is to purchase.

Unfortunately, bad things happen to good people, and no one is exempt. Make sure in your financial planning process that you begin with the end in mind; hope for the best, but plan for the worst.

## Estate Planning

Estate planning is not just for the rich and famous. If you do not have a will (a document expressing how you wish your assets to be distributed upon your death), you are basically asking for trouble and essentially begging the government (of the state you live in) to give away your stuff as they see fit – regardless of your dying wishes.

Not only do we recommend preparing a will, but advise that you consider developing a trust also, which is a prepared document that privately dictates how you'd like your assets to be distributed while you're alive *and* upon your death. The process for creating a Revocable Living Trust involves an attorney who prepares a trust agreement (also called a declaration of trust) which is signed by the settlor and the trustee; and then the settlor transfers property to the trustee to be held for the beneficiary named in the trust document.

A trust is classified as a "living" trust when it is established during the settlor's lifetime and as a "revocable" trust when the settlor has reserved the right to amend or revoke the trust during his or her lifetime. The primary reason for this procedure is because you ALWAYS want to avoid the estate going to probate (high attorney costs, delays, unwanted publicity, court costs, etc). This type of trust does that. Other benefits include the ability to manage funds for heirs for a specified period of time—or until they reach a certain age or level of maturity—and to prevent reckless or irresponsible spending which might put the assets in jeopardy. If the person setting up the estate becomes incapacitated, the trust has built-in provisions for a successor trustee to oversee management of the estate.

While most wills and trusts are future-focused, something few people think about in estate planning is if a parent who is still living becomes the "child" through illness, injury, or disease. In that situation, the child taking over management of the parent's affairs must oversee decisions in the areas of Finances, Medical Care, Benefits, and Key Documents (e.g. health care directives, durable power of attorney, trust documents, living wills, etc.)

If an individual becomes incapacitated and is no longer able to care for him/herself, another trusted individual will need to step in to handle affairs on their behalf. When considering the steps to take to ensure a smooth transition, the following documents should be drawn up to be executed if necessary:

**Durable Power of Attorney** – a written document (not just a verbal agreement or acknowledgment) by which the principal person allows another person (agent, attorney-in-fact, proxy) to act on his/her behalf. The appointee has the power to make key household and financial determinations.

**Durable Power of Attorney for Health Care** – a written document (not just a verbal agreement or acknowledgment) by which the principal person allows another person (agent, attorney-in-fact, proxy) to act on his/her behalf regarding health care and medical treatment issues.

**Living Will** – this document is also known as a "Directive to Physicians" and provides information regarding the types of medical procedures or treatments to be administered or withheld.

It is a very good and worthwhile investment of your time to put in place documents, plans, and procedures to protect your assets from strangers (probate), Uncle Sam (taxes), and time (inflation). In this, the Information and Technology Age, there is no excuse not to have your affairs in order.

The preference for establishing and maintaining up-to-date estate planning documents such as trusts and wills is to have them prepared and reviewed by an attorney. However, there are many other places to get wills and trusts. You can purchase and download software that feature fill-in-the-blank will and trust templates for as little as $20.

Though you might be tempted to spend $20 on software rather than $500 with an attorney, remember that you get what you pay for. Working with a professional who specializes in estate planning will offer ease of process and peace of mind. You don't want to squander away your children's and grandchildren's inheritance because you were too cheap to let a professional protect the assets you worked your entire life to acquire. In the end, it's worth it to make sure you get the best results, take advantage of the most tax breaks, and provide an inheritance for your loved ones. Additionally, over the course of time as your assets increase, a simple online template may not adequately address your financial planning needs. More valuable accounts, legislative and regulatory policy updates, changes in family structure, or other events may require you to update your will or trust. Utilizing the same person and/or firm can help minimize costs and ensure a seamless process.

The objective of *Hope for the Best, Plan for the Worst* is to help you prepare for anything and everything that might arise to derail your life-long efforts to build a good, quality life for you and your family. The priority of all retirement planning, insurance policies, and estate planning is to make sure that you never outlive your money.

## Chapter 14 – Blessed to Be a Blessing

A popular radio host once said, 'Blessed are those who give without remembering; and blessed are those who take without forgetting.'

Do you know why you are blessed with the things you have? Is it so that you can boast and live a comfortable life of convenience? No, we are called to be a blessing to the nations; essentially ambassadors for Jesus. We are called to be distributors of God's wealth. We are called and blessed to actively demonstrate the love of Christ through our living and through our giving. Or, to echo the words of a young minister, 'We can give without loving, but we cannot love without giving.' Yes, indeed, we are blessed to be a blessing which means we have access to various resources for the purpose of helping elevate others in different aspects of their lives. Consider the words of the Lord Jesus himself: 'It is more blessed to give than to receive' (Acts 20:35 ESV).

Blessed to be a blessing is about more than just money. When you are blessed with health, favor, prosperity, and abundance, you are a source of encouragement to others that they too can overcome the challenges and hardships of life. When you are blessed with a quality education, it empowers and motivates others to pursue knowledge for the sake of knowledge, advancement, and mentoring the next generation. When you are blessed with a loving family, it provides a model for others to emulate and to also surround themselves with love and support instead of toxic, negative, and unhealthy relationships. When you are blessed with a spirit of giving and gratitude, it compels other people to follow your example and give to those less fortunate. When others see love in action, it inspires them to act in a like manner.

As believers we should follow the examples routinely demonstrated in scripture. In the Old Testament, when God bestowed blessings upon an individual, He blessed the entire household, blessed the ancestral lineage, and then rained blessings upon the family for multiple generations. When the Bible speaks of savings and inheritances, it instructs us to be a blessing beyond our own lifetime - to think in terms of perpetual blessings, hence, our "children's children." When Jesus returns in full glory to restore His kingdom on earth, it will be for eternity; for those who have accepted Christ and received eternal life through His gift of salvation. God's ultimate plan is to bless us eternally so that we can in return bless and worship Him through our life, love, and service.

Although we have touched on this subject in other chapters, we want to take a moment to expound on a particular verse: *Proverbs 13:22 – "A good man leaves an inheritance for his children's children, but a sinner's wealth is stored up for the righteous."* Proverbs 13:22a, provides an excellent example of a Financial Shepherd. What is clear about this verse is that the wise man leaves a legacy. More often than not though, that legacy does not involve the riches and wealth we tend to think about when we talk about an inheritance. Often the legacy comes in the form of wise counsel and seeds of faithfulness. As the children of Israel benefited from Abraham's faithfulness, and Solomon benefited from David's wise counsel, so too do we have to be prepared to leave an inheritance of righteousness. Most parents want to see their children become more successful than themselves, so they instill in them wisdom from their own life's lessons and other intangible instructions for success. If you were provided with this type of legacy from your own parents, the wisest decision you can make is to work to ingrain the same teaching in your own children, grandchildren, nieces, nephews, and cousins. Truthfully, your children aren't just those that were born to you or reared in your household, they include those that follow your instructions and those that are impacted by your decisions as well.

So, who inherits what you have been fortunate enough to leave behind? The preparation for an inheritance actually starts with the person that has the inheritance to leave. This preparation requires wise counsel as well. There are many examples in the Bible that show the oldest child being the recipient of the majority of the inheritance. Unfortunately, the oldest child may not always be prepared to receive an inheritance due to their own personal circumstances.

Recently we were involved with a family in which this was the case. The matriarch of the family passed away and none of her three adult children was in position to receive the inheritance. Though her assets were not great, she did have the foresight and guidance to elect a beneficiary that she could trust to oversee and execute her wishes as she had planned. The beneficiary happened to be her grandson. Although he was not her biological child, she sowed enough seeds of righteousness in him in advance to prepare him to properly receive and manage this inheritance.

An inheritance should be seen as another way to sow a seed of righteousness in someone's life. Whether you sow through finances, offering services, kindness, gifts, or through prayer, this principal of sowing and reaping has a tremendous impact on the giver(s) as well as the receiver(s).

Your financial purpose in life is to follow God's plan of success for you. This book has been written as a resource to provide information and ideas so that you will be empowered spiritually, emotionally, and financially. You don't have to face your finances alone. Remember, when God is with you, He's also for you; and He is able to do exceeding, abundantly more than you can ask or think.

We want you to recognize that God owns everything. As a result of this, we are expected to be good stewards of the things that He has blessed us with. We have provided some excellent biblical references that support our teachings, and we encourage you to conduct your own independent study on these topics as well. Obviously in this book, our main focus is on money, but this also includes possessions, family, time, talent, treasure, etc… The reader that wants to excel with the least possible risk must first grasp this truth: *The earth and everything in it belongs to God.* This is the foundational premise for a Financial Shepherd. For some, this transition will be simple. They will recognize that this is the change of mindset that we have been talking about throughout this book and furthermore they will acknowledge that this truth stands on its own. Others will recognize that this is true, but choose to continue in their current state of action, because it is more comfortable and it works for them. Yet, many will find this to be the greatest challenge of their lives because it is a natural contradiction to the way they have been taught since birth. Wherever you fall on this spectrum, our hope is that you will choose to be a Financial Shepherd and employ the principles that have been introduced to you in this book.

The concept of *Dollars + Change = Sense* comes with nearly 30 years of combined experience in advising, consulting, counseling, and coaching. During this timeframe, we have worked with clients that were not willing to follow the recommendations we presented based upon their needs and overall goals. Just as some clients have chosen not to make the changes that are necessary to reach their full potential, you too will be faced with the decision to follow or not follow the principles that have been set forth in this book. The following list includes the top five reasons potential clients elected not to follow our proposed recommendations.

1. Fear- Ben Franklin wisely stated, "When you are finished changing, you're finished." From the very moment of our conception until the time of our celestial discharge, we are in a state of constant change. Although it can take on many forms, the truth remains that change is inevitable, and with it comes a natural anxiety that has the potential to be as unsettling as the sea. As a result of fear, many people fail to plan, prepare, and essentially embrace the unavoidable.
2. Stubbornness- "But my people did not listen to my voice; Israel would not submit to me. So I gave them over to their stubborn hearts, to follow their own counsels."- Psalm 81: 11-12 (ESV). As stated in the previous verse, stubbornness is a refusal to listen to wisdom. It is often associated with self-will and can even be confused with persistence. Although both stubbornness and persistence display endurance in the face of resistance, the difference between the two is not always as obvious. As it relates to change, stubbornness is refusing to change something that needs to change, while persistence is making the necessary changes that it takes to achieve a specific goal.
3. Lack of commitment- Truthfully, it is much easier to maintain a non-committal stance because it comes without responsibility. Usually a lack of commitment is preceded by experiences that involve difficulty with trust and loyalty. Positive changes require commitment.
4. Selfishness- Change requires the consideration of the needs of those that are important fixtures in our lives. Unfortunately, many people do not consider the impact of their decisions on those around them. Simply put, failure to plan for the future of those that depend on you displays a blatant disregard for their overall well-being.
5. Poor relationships- The old adage, "You are the company you keep," is especially true when it comes to change. If you lack the support from those that are closest to you, then the

challenge to make and accept change becomes all the more difficult.

After reading this book, if you still don't feel the urge to do anything differently, then you may fall into one of these categories. In *The Financial Shepherd*, we have discussed how to get over and conquer these obstacles so that you will become a better steward for you, your family, and your community.

Reading *The Financial Shepherd* has given you the tools for responsible financial management and stewardship, and demonstrated how to apply those lessons to walk in the blessings of God's financial plan for your life. In addition, we've shared stories, anecdotes, and life lessons to encourage you to walk in greatness based on the divine purpose for your life. We've discussed how to identify and submit to the leadership of a responsible and mature Financial Shepherd whose job is to lead and instruct you in God's principles of financial management. Together, we've discovered how to avoid the pitfalls of debt and how to dig out of a financial ditch. We've reviewed the best options for responsible stewardship over our material wealth and discovered a multitude of avenues that we can use for proper investing that glorifies God and allows us to walk in His divine will. We are now on the road to financial recovery and restoration, financial independence, and success. We wish you the absolute best in your journey, and we will continue to walk down this path toward financial freedom together.

\* \* \*

Glen Wright, II and Sy Pugh

*Money Matters to God*
*[Scriptures are taken from the English Standard Version (ESV)]*

**Psalm 1: 1-3**
Blessed is the man who walks not in the counsel of the wicked, nor stands in the way of sinners, nor sits in the seat of scoffers; but his delight is in the law of the LORD, and on his law he meditates day and night. He is like a tree planted by streams of water that yields its fruit in season, and its leaf does not wither. In all that he does, he prospers.

**Psalm 37:21**
The wicked borrows but does not pay back, but the righteous is generous and gives.

**Proverbs 3:9-10**
Honor the LORD with your wealth and with the firstfruits of all your produce; then your barns will be filled with plenty and your vats will be bursting with new wine.

**Proverbs 10:4**
A slack hand causes poverty, but the hand of the diligent makes rich.

**Proverbs 14:23**
In all toil there is profit, but mere talk tends only to poverty.

**Proverbs 16:8**
Better is a little with righteousness than great revenues with injustice.

**Proverbs 22:4**
The reward for humility and fear of the LORD is riches and honor and life.

**Proverbs 22:7**
The rich rules over the poor, and the borrower is the slave of the lender.

**Proverbs 22:26-27**
Be not one of those who gives pledges, who put up security for debts. If you have nothing with which to pay, why should your bed be taken from under you?

**Proverbs 23:4**
Do not toil to acquire wealth; be discerning enough to desist.

**Proverbs 28:19-20**
Whoever works his land will have plenty of bread, but he who follows worthless pursuits will have plenty of poverty. A faithful man will abound with blessings, but whoever hastens to be rich will not go unpunished.

**Matthew 6:31-33**
Therefore do not be anxious, saying, 'What shall we eat?' or 'What shall we drink?' or 'What shall we wear?' For the Gentiles seek after all these things, and your heavenly Father knows that you need them all. But seek first the kingdom of God and his righteousness, and all these things will be added to you.

**Matthew 7:11**
If you then, who are evil, know how to give good gifts to your children, how much more will your Father who is in heaven give good things to those who ask Him!

**Mark 8:36**
For what does it profit a man to gain the whole world and forfeit his soul?

**Luke 6:38**
Give, and it will be given to you. Good measure, pressed down, shaken together, running over, will be put into your lap. For with the measure you use, it will be measured back to you.

**Luke 16:10**
One who is faithful in a very little is also faithful in much, and one who is dishonest in a very little is also dishonest in much.

**Romans 13:7**
Pay to all what is owed to them: taxes to whom taxes are owed, revenue to whom revenue is owed, respect to whom respect is owed, honor to whom honor is owed.

**2 Corinthians 9:6-8**
The point is this: whoever sows sparingly will also reap sparingly, and whoever sows bountifully will also reap bountifully. Each one must give as he has decided in his heart, not reluctantly or under compulsion, for God loves a cheerful giver. And God is able to make all grace abound to you, so that having all sufficiency in all things at all times, you may abound in every good work.

**Galatians 6:7**
Do not be deceived: God is not mocked, for whatever one sows, that will he also reap.

**1 Timothy 6:9-11**
But those who desire to be rich fall into temptation, into a snare, into many senseless and harmful desires that plunge people into ruin and destruction. For the love of money is a root of all kinds of evils. It is through this craving that some have wandered away from the faith and pierced themselves with many pangs. But as for you, O man of God, flee these things. Pursue righteousness, godliness, faith, love, steadfastness, gentleness.

\* \* \*

*Expand Your Financial Vocabulary*

> $$$ - Here are our recommended Top 50 Terms you should know regarding Financial Investments and Spiritual Returns. Make them a part of your vocabulary:

## BASIC TERMS

1. *Assets* are economic resources. Anything tangible or intangible that is capable of being owned or controlled to produce value and that is held to have positive economic value is considered an asset. Simply stated, assets represent ownership of value that can be converted into cash.
2. *Budgets* are lists of all planned expenses and revenues. Budgets direct the plan for saving and spending based on an estimate of expected incomes and expenses for a given period of time in the future.
3. *Compound interest* is the interest calculated on both the principal and the accrued interest of an investment. Compound interest means that each time interest is paid, it is added to or compounded into the principal amount and thereafter earns interest also.
4. *Financial assessments* are analytical evaluations and metrics used to measure your financial stability and developmental needs, providing broad guidance on approaches, methodologies, and the success/failure of current financial systems.
5. *Financial freedom* provides liberation from financial worries, struggles, and limitations.
6. *Financial independence* is a term generally used to describe the state of having sufficient personal wealth to live indefinitely without having to work actively for basic necessities.
7. *Financial leveraging* is the responsible and acceptable use of credit or external financial resources to gain or increase the value of wealth. Financial Leveraging is not borrowing beyond the ability to pay back, and it is not shifting money from one source to another to cover basic expenses. Financial Leveraging is a tool and process that creates access to opportunities for investment and financial growth.
    a. Good debt
        A financial investment that generates an asset which

will appreciate (go up in value). Good debt is usually tax-deductible.
    b. Bad debt

    A financial decision you know will become a negative, depreciable, or uncollectible debt. Bad debt typically causes harm to your financial status.

8. *Financial literacy* is the ability to understand finances. More specifically, it refers to the set of skills and knowledge that allow an individual to make informed and effective decisions through their understanding of financial terminology, resources, and transactions.

9. *Financial planning* is the long-term process of wisely managing your finances so you can achieve your goals and dreams, while generating a greater return on assets, growth in market share and, and solving foreseeable problems and financial barriers that inevitably arise in every stage of life.

10. *Financial Shepherds* are financially responsible and mature individual(s) in the household accountable for the budget, financial organization and planning, explanations of financial decisions, and financial assessments; individual(s) who monitors household incomes and expenses and shares valuable financial knowledge and information with others as an example of good stewardship.

11. *Inflation* is a rise in the general level of prices of goods and services in an economy over a period of time. When the price level rises, each unit of currency buys fewer goods and services; consequently, inflation is also an erosion in the purchasing power of money.

12. *Liabilities* are current obligations of an entity arising from past transactions or events resulting in moneys owed. Common liabilities include debt which is an amount owed to a person or organization for funds borrowed or on loan. Debt can be represented by a loan note, bond, or mortgage.

13. *Net worth* (sometimes called "net assets") is the total assets minus total liability that determines the value of an individual or company.

14. *Opportunity cost* is an economic term used in business to refer to the value of something given up to pursue something else.

## MONEY MANAGEMENT

15. *Bankruptcy* is a legally declared inability or impairment of ability of an individual or organization to pay debt obligations to creditors.
16. *Entitlements* are a guarantee of access to benefits based on established rights or by legislation. A "right" is itself an entitlement associated with a moral or social principle, such that an "entitlement" is a provision made in accordance with legal framework of a society. In a casual sense, the term "entitlement" refers to a notion or belief that one is deserving of some particular reward or benefit — if given without deeper legal or principled cause, the term is often given with pejorative connotation (e.g. a "sense of entitlement").
17. *Estate Planning* is the process of anticipating and arranging for the dispersal of collective assets. Estate planning typically attempts to eliminate uncertainties over the administration of a probate and maximize the value of the estate by reducing taxes and other expenses.
    a. A will is written documentation of one's personal choices, volition, wish, testament, or bequeath.
    b. Trust involves a fiduciary relationship in which one person (the trustee) holds the title to property (the trust estate or trust property) for the benefit of another (the beneficiary).
18. *Gifts* are something given voluntarily without expecting payment in return, as to show favor toward someone, honor an occasion, or make a gesture of assistance.
19. *Giving* is to present something voluntarily and without expecting compensation; to bestow upon. Financially speaking, sowing and giving generously are vital components of the Financial Shepherding process.
20. *Progress/Status Report* informs an individual in a position of accountability (financial planner, financial shepherd, supervisor, associate, or customer) about the work accomplished on a project or task over a certain period of time.
21. *Savings* represents the total accumulated amount of income that is not spent on consumption but is preserved or set aside for future use. Savings is income not spent; or deferred consumption. Methods of saving include putting money

aside in a bank or pension plan. Saving also includes reducing expenditures, such as recurring costs. In terms of personal finance, saving specifies low-risk preservation of money, as in a deposit account, versus investment, wherein risk is higher.
22. *Stewardship* is the ability of one to effectively and profitably manage his or her property, finances, or other affairs.
23. *Systematic Savings* is a process to help you save regularly. It is just like a recurring deposit with a credit union or bank where you put in a small amount every month. The difference here is that the amount is invested, commonly in a mutual fund. Usually a minimum deposit is required.
24. *Tithing* represents a gift of the first one-tenth part of something, paid as a voluntary contribution or as a tax or levy, usually to support a religious organization. From a Christian perspective, the tithe represents honor and obedience to God.

## CHARACTERISTICS & TRAITS

25. *Blessings* (also used to refer to bestowing of such) are the infusion of something with holiness, divine will, or one's hope or approval. Something promoting or contributing to happiness, well-being, or prosperity.
26. *Character* is the aggregate of features and traits that form the individual nature of some person or thing as well as the combination of qualities or features that distinguishes one person, group, or thing from another. Character also refers to the state of moral excellence and integrity.
27. *Ethics* is a law philosophy that addresses questions about morality — that is, concepts such as good and evil, right and wrong, justice, virtue, etc. Ethics are considered the moral standards by which people judge behavior.
28. *Faith* is confident belief in the truth, value, or trustworthiness of a person, idea, or thing.
29. *Integrity* encompasses steadfast adherence to a strict moral or ethical code. Integrity is a concept of consistency of actions, values, methods, measures, principles, expectations, and outcomes. In western ethics, integrity is regarded as the quality of having an intuitive sense of honesty and truthfulness in regard to the motivations for one's actions.
30. *Intelligence* is an umbrella term describing a property of the

mind including related abilities, such as the capacities for abstract thought, understanding, communication, reasoning, learning, learning from past experiences, planning, and problem-solving. The faculty of thought and reason with the capacity to acquire and apply knowledge.

31. *Learned Behaviors* are behaviors that are observed and employed by an individual that finds them to be beneficial in some way as a result of an associated motivating factor; said behaviors also can be conditioned. Learned behaviors are conditioned responses to stimuli through either voluntary or involuntary intents.
32. *Patience* is the state of endurance under difficult circumstances, which can mean persevering in the face of delay or provocation without acting on annoyance/anger in a negative way; or exhibiting forbearance when under strain, especially when faced with longer-term difficulties.
33. *Poor* means having little or no wealth and few or no possessions, money, goods, or other means of support; usually relying on charity or public support.
34. *Rich* refers to possessing many material goods of value; abundantly supplied with resources, means, or funds.
35. *Self Awareness* is a mental and emotional cognizance of oneself, including one's traits, feelings, and behaviors. Self-awareness is the state or ability to perceive, to feel, or to be conscious of events, objects or sensory patterns of one's being.
36. *Trustworthy* refers to reliance and dependability on someone or something worthy of confidence.
37. *Wealthy* is possessing an abundance of valuable resources such as good mental/emotional/physical health and general contentment in life; including material possessions or the control of such assets; affluent.

## PLANNING & PREPARATION

38. *American Dream* is often used in the context of "Chasing the American Dream," representing a national ethos of the United States in which freedom includes a promise of prosperity and success. The idea of the American Dream is rooted in the second sentence of the United States Declaration of Independence which states that "all men are created equal"

and that they are "endowed by their Creator with certain inalienable Rights" including "Life, Liberty and the Pursuit of Happiness."

39. *Insurance* includes the act, system, or business of protecting property, life, one's person, etc., against loss or harm arising in specified contingencies (e.g. fire, accident) with a promise of compensation for specific potential future losses in exchange for a periodic payment.

    a. Life insurance is a contract between the policy owner and the insurer, where the insurer agrees to pay a designated beneficiary a sum of money upon the occurrence of the insured individual's or individuals' death or other event, such as terminal illness or critical illness. In return, the policy owner agrees to pay a stipulated amount at regular intervals or in lump sums.

    b. Long-term care insurance is an insurance product sold by a licensed agent and helps provide for the cost of long-term care beyond a predetermined period. Long-term care insurance covers care generally not covered by health insurance, Medicare, or Medicaid. Individuals who require long-term care are generally not sick in the traditional sense, but instead, are unable to perform the basic activities of daily living such as dressing, bathing, eating, toileting, continence, transferring (getting in and out of a bed or chair), and walking.

    c. Disability insurance is a form of insurance that insures the beneficiary's earned income against the risk that disability will make working (and therefore earning) impossible. It includes paid sick leave, short-term disability benefits, and long-term disability benefits.

    d. Property & Casualty insurance protects policyholders in the event of damage to their property (theft, fire, or vandalism) or from liability that occurs on or in the use of their property. Property and casualty insurance is available for both business and personal property and can be purchased from insurance agents who are licensed to sell the products in a particular state.

    e. Health insurance is insurance against loss by illness

or bodily injury. Health insurance provides coverage for medicine, visits to the doctor or emergency room, hospital stays, and other medical expenses. Policies differ in what they cover, the size of the deductible and/or co-payment, limits of coverage and the options for treatment available to the policyholder. Health insurance can be directly purchased by an individual, or it may be provided through an employer. Medicare and Medicaid are programs which provide health insurance to elderly, disabled, or un-insured individuals.
40. *Legacy* is something that is passed down from one period of time to another period of time; transferred from an ancestor or predecessor. A historical legacy can be a positive thing or a negative thing – in the form of tangible or intangible items such as philosophies or ideologies. Personal legacies refer to one's ability to leave behind a positive and substantive memory of significant accomplishment or achievement to be passed on.
41. *Retirement* is removal or withdrawal from one's occupation, service, office, or business. It represents a general transition from full-time employment or activity in the workforce into part-time endeavors including work or recreation. Often retirement income is derived from savings, investments, pensions, or dividends, etc.
42. *Vision* is the act or power of anticipating that which will or may come to be. A vision can be political, religious, environmental, social, or technological in nature. A visionary is a person with a clear, distinctive, and specific vision of the future and potential implications for advances in business, technology, religion, or social/political endeavors.

## INVESTING

43. *Index Investing* is an investment strategy that does not require active trading and is used as a smaller sample of the market that is representative of the whole. Investors use indexes to track the performance of the stock market. Ideally, a change in the price of an index represents an exactly proportional change in the stocks included in the index.

44. *Investment Tools*
   a. *Annuities* are contracts typically sold by an insurance company designed to provide payments to the holder at specified intervals, usually after retirement.
   b. *Bonds* are a debt security, similar to an I.O.U. When you purchase a bond, you are lending money to a government, municipality, corporation, federal agency, or other entity known as an issuer. In return for that money, the issuer provides you with a bond in which it promises to pay a specified rate of interest during the life of the bond and to repay the face value of the bond (the principal) when it matures, or comes due.
   c. *Commodities* are goods for which there is demand. Commodities are substances, basic resources, and agricultural products that come out of the earth and maintain roughly a universal price. They are fungible, i.e. equivalent no matter who produces them. Prices are universal based on global supply and demand.
   d. *Mutual Funds* are open-ended funds operated by an investment company which raises money from shareholders and invests in a group of assets, in accordance with a stated set of objectives. Mutual funds raise money by selling shares of the fund to the public, much like any other type of company can sell stock in itself to the public. In return for the money they give to the fund when purchasing shares, shareholders receive an equity position in the fund and, in effect, in each of its underlying securities. Mutual funds offer choice, liquidity, and convenience, but charge fees and often require a minimum investment.
   e. *Real Estate* is land, including all the natural resources and permanent buildings on it, along with improvements to the land, such as buildings, fences, structures and other site improvements that are fixed in location.
   f. *Stocks* represent a claim on a company's assets and earnings. They are instruments that signify an ownership position (called equity) in a corporation and represent a claim on its proportional share in the corporation's assets and profits. Ownership in

the company is determined by the number of shares (stocks) a person owns divided by the total number of shares outstanding.
45. *Real Rate of Return* represents the annual percentage return realized on an investment, which is adjusted for changes in prices due to inflation or other external effects.
46. *Risk Tolerance* is the degree of uncertainty that an investor can handle in regard to a negative change in the value of his or her portfolio varying according to age, income requirements, financial goals, etc.

## WISE COUNSELORS

47. *Board of Directors* functions as the governing body of an incorporated firm whose members are elected normally by the subscribers (stockholders) of the firm (generally at an annual general meeting) to govern the firm and look after the subscribers' interests. The board has the ultimate decision-making authority and, in general, is empowered to set the company's policy, objectives, and overall direction. It is recommended that a personal board of directors be incorporated into an individual's financial planning process.
48. *Certified Financial Planner* is the professional certification mark for financial planners conferred by the Certified Financial Planner Board of Standards Inc. in the United States. To receive authorization to use the CFP designation, the candidate must meet education, examination, experience, and ethics requirements, and pay an ongoing certification fee.
49. *Counseling* or *Wise Counsel* is advice, information, warning, guidance or admonition that provides direction as to a decision or course of action. Advice or guidance, especially as solicited from a knowledgeable person, through an act of exchanging opinions and ideas.
50. *The Chief Financial Shepherd:* Each Financial Shepherd understands that s/he is to give account of his stewardship to the Chief Financial Shepherd, Jesus Christ.

\* \* \*

## NATIONAL CREDIT REPORTING AGENCIES

EQUIFAX INFORMATION SERVICES
P.O. BOX 740256
ATLANTA, GA 30374
800-685-1111
WWW.EQUIFAX.COM

EXPERIAN
P.O. BOX 2002
ALLEN, TX 75013
888-397-3742
WWW.EXPERIAN.COM

TRANSUNION
P.O. BOX 1000
CHESTER, PA 19022
800-888-4213
WWW.TRANSUNION.COM

Recommended Resources:
*Online*
Investopedia – www.investopedia.com
NASDAQ – www.nasdaq.com
Wall Street Journal – www.wsj.com
Zacks Investment Research – www.zacks.com

*Magazines*
Kiplinger
Money

*Indices*
Barclays Capital Aggregate Bond Index
Dow Jones Industrial Average
NASDAQ Composite Index
Russell 2000
Standard and Poor's 500 Stock Composite Index

## Bibliography

"consciousness." *Merriam-Webster Online Dictionary*. 2010. http://www.merriam-webster.com (August 2010).

*English Standard Version Bible*. Wheaton: Crossway Bibles, Good News Publishers, 2008. <http://www.esv.org>

*The Holy Bible*: King James Version. Uhrichsville: Barbour Publishing, 2003. Print.

National Vital Statistics System. National Center of Health Statistics. Atlanta, Centers for Disease Control and Prevention. 2007. <www.cdc.gov/nchs/>

"Poverty Guidelines, Research & Management." U.S. Department of Health and Human Services, 2009. <http://aspe.hhs.gov/poverty/09extension.shtml>

"Retirement Planning." Worth Financial Advisory Group. 2010.

Simon, Mashaun D. "U.S. Minimum Wage Doesn't Cover Family Living Costs, Study Says." Bloomberg Press. July 2004.

"Suddenly Single" – *Financial Psychology and Lifechanging Events*. Greenwood Village: National Endowment for Financial Education, 2004.

www.psychpage.com

www.ingramcontent.com/pod-product-compliance
Lightning Source LLC
Chambersburg PA
CBHW032017170526
45157CB00002B/742